La
WESTERN
CRETE

a countryside guide

Tenth edition

Jonnie Godfrey
and
Elizabeth Karslake

SUNFLOWER BOOKS

Tenth edition © 2023
Sunflower Books™
PO Box 36160
London SW7 3WS, UK
www.sunflowerbooks.co.uk

ISBN 978-1-85691-546-5

Craft shop at Topolia (Walk 16, Car tour 1)

Important note to the reader

We have done our best to ensure that the descriptions and maps in this book are error-free at press date. The book will be updated, where necessary, in future editions. It is always very helpful for us to receive your comments (sent in care of info@sunflowerbooks.co.uk, please) for the updating of future editions.

We also rely on those who use this book — especially walkers — to take along a good supply of common sense when they explore. Conditions change fairly rapidly on Crete, and ***storm damage or bulldozing may make a route unsafe at any time***. If the route is not as we outline it here, and your way ahead is not secure, return to the point of departure. ***Never attempt to complete a tour or walk under hazardous conditions!*** Please read carefully the notes on pages 41-49, as well as the introductory comments at the beginning of each tour and walk (regarding road conditions, equipment, grade, distances and time, etc). Explore ***safely***, while at the same time respecting the beauty of the countryside.

Cover photograph: Samaria Gorge
Title page: Agia Sophia cave chapel in the Topolia Gorge

Photos: Elizabeth Karslake, with the exception of pages 137, 147: Tanya Tsikas; 37, 142-3: Footscapes of Crete; 84: Annapeletzidou and 138-9: C Messier (both CC BY SA 4.0 via Wikimedia Commons); 4, 81, 83, 91, 92, 94 (top right), 101 (bottom): Jan Kostura; 2, 12-3, 20-1, 35, 43, 65, 73, 75, 76, 79, 89, 94 (top left and bottom), 97, 106: Robert Lefever; 15, 18-9, 22-3, 24, 28-9, 32-3, 36-7, 38, 39, 52, 55, 63, 68-9, 82-3, 110 (top), 115, 118, 128, 129, 138-9, 148 and cover (Shutterstock); 59: Sharon Rochford drawings
Maps: Nick Hill for Sunflower Books. Base map data © OpenStreetMap contributors. Contour data made available under ODbL (opendata commons.org/licenses/odbl/1.0)
A CIP catalogue record for this book is available from the British Library.
Printed and bound in England: Short Run Press, Exeter

Contents

THE WALKS

Beautiful stone-laid trail to Moni Katholikou and the sea (Walk 11)

Preface

Mountains rearing straight up from the sea, deep wooded gorges, ravines and valleys — and yet more glorious mountains, standing proud and acting as a magnet to the eye and the imagination — that's Western Crete, or real Crete, as some would say. Its strong, dramatic scenery and colours create sweeping landscapes of harsh but beautiful countryside — countryside that has been the backdrop for heroic deeds, ancient civilisations and constant intrigue for thousands of years, and the home of obdurate, tough-spirited people — made so by their labours on the land and their experiences.

Getting to know Western Crete takes time; the number of people who explore beyond the obvious is slowly growing. We hope we will lead you straight to the heart of the matter with this book, whether you are a first- or second-time visitor unsure about how best to get to know the island or, indeed, if you are someone who doesn't need convincing but would like a reliable, thorough and different guide. We encourage you to explore to the full. We won't need to inspire you; one look at Western Crete will do that.

Landscapes of Western Crete, in the same tried and tested format as the other titles in the 'Landscapes' Series, takes you well off the beaten track, while at the same time describing in full the most popular touring routes and excursions. This Tenth edition is a thorough update and in a wider — we hope more readable — format.

Everyone has heard of the Samaria Gorge, and rightly so. But frankly, anyone who contemplates walking the gorge — a long and by no means unchallenging expedition — could accomplish a number of other walks in this book and gain a great amount of pleasure in alternative landscapes. What's more, walking almost anywhere else in Western Crete will give the added bonus of solitude and perhaps an even greater feeling for the island and its people, who vary both in style and character from region to region.

Acknowledging the fact that Western Crete attracts a number of visitors who choose to have more than one base, or who don't feel obliged to return to their villa, hotel or apartment every night, we have described walks that can be linked and which cover a large expanse of the western end of the island. Western Crete lends itself to this arrangement very well. These walks start on the shoulders of the awe-inspiring

Elizabeth (left) and Jonnie — on the ground in Crete when writing the first editions of Eastern and Western Crete

White Mountains *(Levka Ori)* — even when they're not snow-capped, their peaks are a striking white, hence their name — and descend to the south coast, from where you can head either west or east.

We have been asked, often, if and how western and eastern Crete differ from one another. In fact we naturally made the comparison ourselves in the course of compiling this guide, having previously written *Landscapes of Eastern Crete*. The west is even more mountainous and has developed more slowly than the east; the geography is such that walks tend to be longer and the terrain, on the whole, rougher in the west. And the people of Western Crete are somewhat more reserved than their counterparts in the east. Western Crete has its own captivating and entrancing character. You simply need to immerse yourself in the countryside to find out.

— JONNIE GODFREY

Acknowledgements

Many thanks to all the users who send us helpful updates, to the friends who initially hiked with us, to Liz and Paul Marsden of Footscapes of Crete for help with the Seventh edition, and to Mike Hyde who followed in our footsteps with his GPS and logged the original GPS tracks for this guide. For this Tenth edition we are particularly grateful to Jan Kostura who checked readers' emails post-pandemic, as well as walks damaged by the storms of 2019 and 2020, while preparing the Tour & Trail map mentioned on page 14.

Background reading

John Bowman: *The Travellers' Guide: Crete*
Pat Cameron: *Blue Guide Crete*
David MacNeil Doren: *The Winds of Crete* (John Murray)
Adam Hopkins: *Crete: Past, Present & Peoples* (Faber)
Nikos Kazantzakis: *Zorba the Greek* (Faber)
Patrick Leigh Fermor: *Abducting a General* (John Murray)
W Stanley Moss: *Ill Met by Moonlight* (Buchan and Enwright)
Oleg Polunin: *Flowers of the Mediterranean* (Chatto)
Oliver Rackham and Jennifer Moody: *The Making of the Cretan Landscape* (Manchester University Press)

Getting about

Hiring a car is certainly one of the best ways to get to know Crete. We hope that by giving you some good itineraries, you will be able to make the most of the island — and your car. Many of the tours we suggest will take you past the starting- and/or end-points of several walks. In fact, seeing the countryside from a car will encourage you, we hope, to go off the beaten track and into the hills with us, on foot.

Taxis are an alternative way to tour and, if shared, can be a reasonably-priced way to travel. Do agree a fare before setting out, if it's going to be an unmetered trip. If necessary, your holiday company's agent or representative will help you to find a driver who speaks English and who will be happy and proud to show off his island.

Organised excursions are good value; coaches eat up the kilometres while you sit back and watch it all go by.

One of the best ways of getting about is by **local bus**. Once you've done it for the first time, you'll realise it's economical, reliable and entertaining. You'll whizz along the highways and bumble through villages with a bus-eye view over the countryside. Use the local bus network to explore Western Crete economically.

The plans overleaf locate the bus stations in Hania and Rethimnon. Timetables for buses covering the western half of the island are on pages 149-150. A good website (in English) for Hania's urban buses is chaniabus.gr. ***Note:*** *Even if you have downloaded timetables from the web (see page 149), do pick up a current bus timetable* at the station before you plan any excursions: the frequency of services changes with the seasons. For complete assurance, verify the times in advance by asking.

If you are lucky, the officials at Hania bus station (where, incidentally, there is a left luggage facility) will tell you the number of the bus you want; arrive in good time, as buses leave promptly and sometimes even *earlier* than scheduled, particularly those that depart at the crack of dawn. Most tickets are bought at the depot before boarding, including those to Samaria (the 'Omalos' bus). If you *do* buy tickets on the bus, don't be confused if you get three per person for just one trip — they add up to the total. You can flag down buses en route, but they don't always stop. *Always* put your hand out, even at a bus stop.

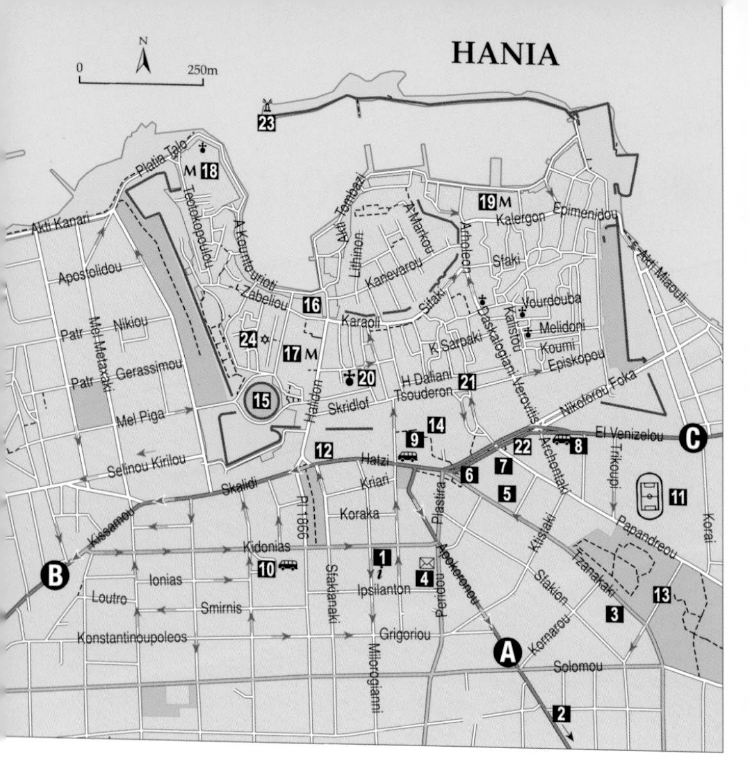

HANIA — KEY

1 Tourist information bureau
2 Tourist police (L Irakliou)
3 Greek Alpine Club (EOS)
4 Post office
5 Telephone and internet (Cosmote)
6 National Bank of Greece
7 Bank of Greece
8 for Akrotiri
9 for Akrotiri, Iraklion, Souda, Mournies and town routes
10 Bus station: for Alikianos, Aptera (beach), Hora Sfakion, Kalamaki, Kandanos, Kastelli-Kissamos, Lakki, Meskla, Omalos (Samaria), Paleohora, Platanias (beach), Platanos, Rethimnon, Sougia, Xiloskala (Samaria)
11 Stadium
12 Piraeus Bank
13 Public gardens and zoo
14 Market
15 Shivao bastion
16 Al Hammam (traditional baths)
17 Folklore museum
18 Maritime museum (Firka tower)
19 Venetian shipyards
20 Cathedral
21 Minaret
22 Taxi rank
23 Venetian lighthouse
24 Synagogue

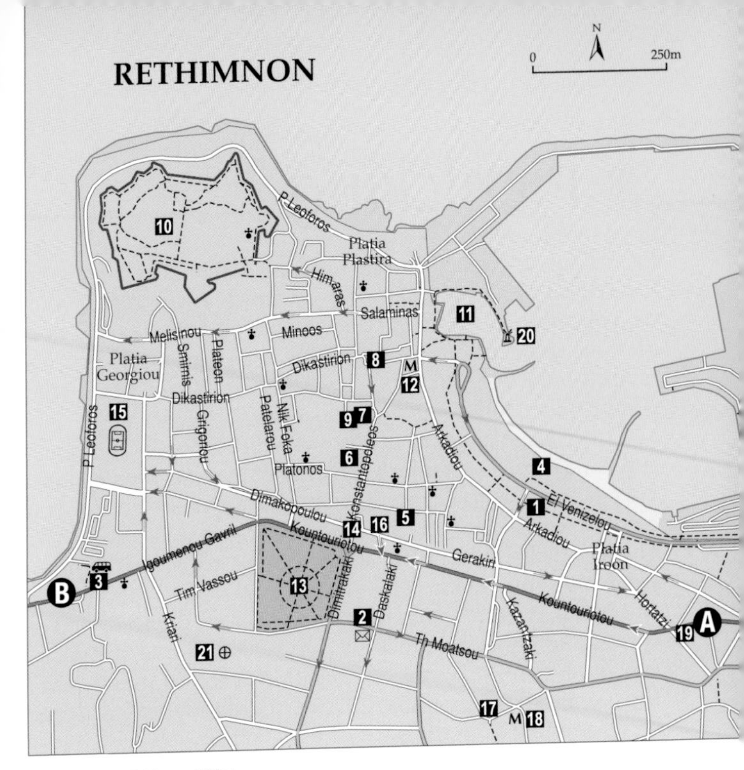

RETHIMNON — KEY

1 Tourist information bureau
2 Post office
3 Bus station
4 Public beach
5 Youth hostel
6 Archaeological museum
7 Nerantzes mosque
8 Rimondi fountain
9 Nerantzes fountain
10 Venetian fortress
11 Venetian harbour
12 Museum (Venetian loggia)
13 Public gardens
14 Porta Guora
15 Stadium
16 Taxi rank
17 Telephone and internet (OTE)
18 Paleontological museum
19 National Bank of Greece
20 Lighthouse
21 Hospital

Picnicking

Picnicking on Crete is not an organised affair. There are very few specially-provided sites; it's very much a case of pick your own olive tree and toss for the best view. Following is a selection of some good places to throw down a towel or a rug (it's unlikely to be wet, but it might well be prickly) and revel in the countryside. Don't forget the corkscrew ...

These picnic suggestions have been chosen for ease of access, and none involves too much climbing or lugging of provisions. We tell you how to get there (including waypoints so that you can set your satnav if you like) and how long a walk you'll have. Naturally, all these picnic strolls can be extended to make satisfying short walks.

Note that *picnic numbers correspond to walk numbers:* on the corresponding *walking* map the precise location of the picnic spot is shown on by the symbol **P**, printed in green. (The three suggestions prefixed 'CT' are specifically linked to the corresponding car tours.)

All picnickers should read the Country code on page 13 and go quietly in the countryside.

1 Agia Lake *(map page 51; photos on pages 52, 53); **allow 5-30min on foot***
Following Car tour 3, from **Agia** drive towards 'KIRTOMADOS' and park on the track to the lake, just beyond a bridge with iron railings (35° 28.632'N, 23° 55.788'E). Now it's only 5min to a pleasant spot by the lake. For a longer walk, park on the main road in **Agia** (35° 28.346'N, 23° 55.854'E) and follow the Short walk on page 50.

These pleasant hillsides below Polirinia are the setting for Picnic 14.

2 Kotsifou Gorge *(map page 56, photo on page 55)*; ***allow about 40min on foot***
🚗 Following Car tour 3, park in **Plakias** (35° 11.423'N, 24° 23.714'E). Follow Short walk 2 on page 54 to the GORGE and MILL.

3 Diktamos Gorge *(map pages 56-57, photo on page 58)*; ***allow 5-15min on foot***
🚗 Follow Car tour 5. Coming downhill into **Katohori**, on a big U-bend to the right (by a miniature concrete church), take the road to the left. Continue 400m to a small square and park (35° 26.285'N, 24° 3.947'E).Then follow Walk 3, page 56 and either picnic at the small PICNIC SITE (under 5min) or in the GORGE itself (from about 15min).

4 Kambi *(map page 62)*; ***allow 10-30min on foot***
🚗 Follow Car tour 5 and park in **Kambi** near the church (35° 25.078'N, 24° 4.178'E). Then follow Walk 4 (page 60) as far as the PICNIC AREA below on the right.

6 Kournas Lake *(map page 67, photos on pages 68-69)*; ***allow about 10min on foot***
🚗 Nearing the end of Car tour 6 you pass **Lake Kournas**. Either park on the main road or drive down towards the lake (free parking). Just find a nice spot or use the map and notes for Walk 6 to stretch your legs.

9 Rethimnon *(map page 77)*; ***allow up to 5min on foot***
🚗 Car tours 6, 7, and 8 take you to **Rethimnon**. From the town drive up towards the chapel of Profitis Ilias. To get there, head south uphill at the eastern side of town on the road to Roussospiti (Theotokopoulou Street). The chapel itself is inaccessible, but there is good picnicking to the left, just past the motorway, or a short way further up, in the PINES — off a steep road just before the track to the chapel.

10 Myli Gorge *(map page 80, photos on pages 43 and 81)*; ***allow about 10min on foot***
🚗 Car tours 6, 7, and 8 take you to **Rethimnon**. From there **Myli** and its gorge can be reached as a detour either via Roussospiti or via Perivolia (see the map on page 80; 35° 20.258'N, 24° 30.236'E). Follow Walk 10 on page 80 for as long as you like.

14 Polirinia *(map page 91, photo opposite)*; ***allow 20-25min on foot***
🚗 Follow Car tour 1 and take the DETOUR TO **Polirinia**. Park near the taverna at the end of the road (35° 27.305'N, 23° 39.040'E) and use the map to walk south out of the village. Picnic just past the last houses.

15 Katsomatados *(map page 94, photo on page 94)*; ***allow under 10min on foot***
🚗 Follow Car tour 1 to **Katsomatados**, 3km south of Topolia (35° 24.328'N, 23° 40.933'E). Then use notes on page 92 to picnic near the start of Walk 15.

18 Sougia *(map pages 100-101, photos on pages 89)*; ***allow about 10-15min on foot***
🚗 Following Car tour 3, park in **Sougia** (35° 14.828'N, 23° 48.423'E). Use the notes for Walk 18 on page 101 to picnic in the GORGE.

26 Imbros Gorge *(map page 128, photo on page 129)*; ***allow about 20min on foot***
🚗 Follow Car tour 6 to the ENTRANCE TO THE GORGE and park (35° 15.231'N, 24° 10.281'E). Then use notes on page 127 to start Walk 26. If you go far enough into the gorge, you may have to pay.

28 Megalopotamos River *(map page 136, photo below)*
allow under 5min on foot

Follow Car tour 6 past **Asomatos**, to the arched BRIDGE over the Megalopotamos River (35° 10.441'N, 24° 27.958'E). Picnic here, or at the pools below it.

29 Kaloidena Chapel *(map page 140)*; ***allow 5min to 20min on foot***

Follow Car tour 8 to **Ano Meros** and park (35° 11.237'N, 24° 39.659'E). Then follow the first 20min of Walk 29 (page 138) to the pretty chapel with its spring and picnic area. Or *drive* there: follow the road from Ano Meros towards HORDAKI, then turn right uphill at the brown sign-post 'KALOIDENA MONASTERY'.

32 Eleftherna *(map page 148, photo on page 147)*; ***allow under 10min to 1h on foot***

Drive from Rethimnon (Car tours 6, 7, 8) to **Archaia Eleftherna** (35° 19.416'N, 24° 40.590'E). Follow Walk 32 (page 146) to picnic at the BYZANTINE TOWER — or go as far as you like (the HELLENISTIC BRIDGE reached in 1h is a particularly pleasant setting).

CT4 Moni Gouverneto *(touring map and map page 83)*; ***allow 5-10min on foot***

Follow Car tour 4 to **Moni Gouverneto** (35° 35.075'N, 24° 8.406'E) There are good places on the hillside below the monastery, but little shade.

CT6 Kourtaliotiko Gorge *(touring map and map page 119)*; ***5min down on foot, 10min up***

Follow Car tour 6 from **Asomatos** (page 31); park 600m along the gorge (35° 11.659'N, 24° 27.830'E), to picnic at the **Agios Nikolaos** chapel.

CT8 Amari Valley *(touring map)*; ***allow under 5min on foot***

From the south side of the **Platys River** (125.5km on Car tour 8, page 40) take the slip road down to the ARCHED BRIDGE to picnic (35° 10.371'N, 24° 41.708'E).

Country code for walkers and motorists

Observance of certain unwritten rules is essential when out walking or driving in the countryside anywhere, but especially on Crete's rugged terrain, where irresponsible behaviour can lead to dangerous mistakes. Whether you are an experienced rambler or not, it is important to adhere to a country code, to avoid causing damage, harming animals, or even endangering your own life.

- **Do not light fires**; everything gets tinder dry.
- **Do not frighten animals.** The goats and sheep you may encounter are not used to strangers. By making a noise, trying to touch or photograph them, you may cause them to run in fear and be hurt.
- **Walk quietly** through all farms, hamlets and villages, and leave all gates just as you found them, wherever they are. Although animals may not be in evidence, the gates *do* have a purpose.
- **Protect all wild and cultivated plants.** Don't pick fruit if it looks like it is somebody else's livelihood. You'll doubtless be offered some en route, anyhow. Avoid walking over cultivated land.
- **Take all your litter** away.
- When **driving**, never block roads or tracks. Park where you will not inconvenience anyone or cause danger.

And especially for walkers:

- **Do not take risks.** Do not attempt walks beyond your capacity and do not wander off the paths described if there is any sign of gathering mist or if it is late in the day.
- **Do not walk alone** and *always* tell a responsible person *exactly* where you are going and when you plan to return. On any but a very short walk near villages, take a mobile, GPS or compass, whistle, torch, extra water and warm clothing, as well as some high energy food, like chocolate. Although this may sound 'over the top' to an inexperienced walker, it could save your life.

This lovely bridge over the Megalopotamos river is just one setting where you could enjoy Picnic 28, especially at the shaded river below — where you'll have some geese for company. Another potential picnic spot on this road is at the ruined monastery shown at the bottom of page 35 — which may be less crowded.

Touring

Crete is a very large island, and most visitors hire a car for some part of their stay to try to get to grips with it.

It pays to hire for a minimum of three days and, while you may find cheaper rates with smaller firms, remember that the larger companies offer the advantage of representation all over the island. Since it's likely that you'll want to cover a lot of ground, you'll be in a better position with a well-known company should anything go wrong.

For general touring covering the whole island, Sunflower recommends the **Michelin** map (1:140,000). To get off the beaten track, we have been using the 1:100,000 maps 'Central Crete' and 'Western Crete' published by **Terrain Cartography**, but *beware:* their 'smooth dirt road' is usually only suitable for 4WD! But we await publication of the **Tour & Trail** map for Western Crete at a scale of 1:40,000! Remember that your car hire contact will no doubt prohibit off-road driving and that **tyres** are *not* covered by insurance; you won't be charged for a simple puncture, but ruined tyres will have to be paid for! Be sure you understand the terms of the hire contract. Keep your hire contract, passport and driving licence with you at all times when out on the road. Take note of the hire company's telephone numbers (both office hours and *out of hours*), just in case. **Petrol** is widely available, but it is still a good idea to set out with plenty.

Our car touring notes are brief; they include little information readily available in standard guidebooks or the handouts you can obtain free from tourist offices and tourist information kiosks at home or on Crete. Instead, we've concentrated on the 'logistics' of touring: times and distances, road conditions, and giving clear directions where you might falter or be misled — for instance, by lack of signposting. Most of all, we emphasise possibilities for **walking** and **picnicking**. While some of the suggestions for short walks and picnics may not be suitable during a long car tour, you may find a landscape that you would like to explore at leisure another day. (Note that references in brackets at the top of a tour refer to walks and picnics that can be easily reached by *detouring* off the main route.)

Our pull-out touring maps are ideal for planning and in fact contain all the information you will need outside the towns. The tours have been written up with Hania as departure/return point, but can quite easily be joined from other centres. Plans of Hania and Rethimnon are on pages 8-9.

SOME POINTS WORTH NOTING

We cannot stress too strongly the advantage of taking with you a good guide to Crete's history and archaeological heritage; see page 6. Note also:

- **Allow plenty of time for visits**; our times for the tours include only very brief stops at viewpoints labelled (📷) in the notes.
- **Telephones** (should you need one) are located at most kiosks, at OTE (telephone exchanges) and in *cafeneions*. Many telephone boxes are card phones; buy cards at kiosks. Calls are metered.
- WC indicates **public toilets**; these are rare, but others are found in restaurants.
- Don't be flummoxed by **Greek road signs**; they are almost invariably followed by English ones.
- You are meant to cross a **solid white line near the edge of the road**, when someone wants to overtake. However, beware of slower vehicles, laden donkeys, bikes, etc ahead, when you round corners.
- Conversely, **a solid white line in the middle of the road** means NO OVERTAKING — despite the behaviour of motorists who appear not to notice it.
- **Do think** before you pull up to admire a view, if you are not at a viewpoint with parking; remember that other motorists cannot see round corners.
- Never throw **cigarette ends** out of the car.
- Come to a standstill at **stop signs**.
- The spelling of **village names** may vary. We have used the letter 'H' where an 'X' or 'CH' might be used locally; this is to aid pronunciation.
- In towns, only **park** your car where permitted.
- In villages it may be difficult to locate the **through road** which may be narrow and unsigned.
- **Priority signs** (red/black/white arrows) on narrow roads give priority to the *black* arrow.

- You will see many **shrines** beside the road (they vary from little boxes topped by a cross and filled with oil, a candle, icon or pictures to very elaborate miniature churches like the one shown above). They warn travellers that sometime in the past a fatal or near-fatal accident involving motor vehicles has occurred at that spot. **Drive carefully!**

Distances quoted are *cumulative kilometres* from Hania. A key to the symbols in the notes is on the touring map. Do note, however, that only the largest churches — or churches that are landmarks — have been highlighted, since every village has at least one church. The same can be said of tavernas or *cafeneions;* food and drink can be found almost anywhere.

All motorists should read the Country code on page 13 and go quietly in the countryside. ***Kalo taxithee!***

Car tour 1: THE FAR WEST

Hania • (Kastelli-Kissamos) • (Polirinia) • Vathi • Moni Chrisoskalitisas • (Elafonisi) • Elos • Topolia • Hania

164km/102mi; about 5 hours' driving; Exit B from Hania (town plan page 8). We use the old north coast road to begin, not the A90 highway. All roads are quite good.

Walks en route: 1, (12), (13), (14), 15, 16, (19)
Picnic suggestions (see pages 10-13): (14 at Polirinia), 15 at Katsomatados

Western Crete is renowned for its beautiful beaches, but this comes at the price of crowds arriving in coachloads. No doubt you will be urged to visit Balos, the mesmerising lagoon shown opposite: it's certainly worth seeing, but getting there by car or by boat is going to eat up most of a day. On this tour you have the option of visiting another gorgeous beach, equally crowded, before immersing yourself in the countryside on the return leg.

From 1866 Square, take Exit B (Skalidi, then Kissamou). There will be plenty of petrol stations along the north coast road, so fill up (⛽) before turning off. Very shortly past the turning left to Theriso (1.2km) you come to a large Y-fork: be sure to keep straight on here for 'PLATANIAS', leaving the route to Omalos and the A90 national highway off to the left. Continue west on the old north coast road. All the beach-side villages on this route — **Galatas, Kalamaki, Glaros, Kato Stalos** (where Walk 1 begins and ends), **Agia Marina**, **Platanias** — have tavernas and rooms and apartments for rent (▲▲△✕).

Cross the Keritis River (12km) and drive on (⛽ 13.6km), flanked by orange groves and large patches of bamboo (⛽ 15.5km). Soon the route passes through **Maleme** (16km ▲✕⛽). The village saw violent activity during the Second World War; it was here that the Battle of Crete flared up. At 17km you pass the Mike Hotel on the right; the first turning left past the hotel, signposted to Vlacheronista, leads to the German War Graves (also signposted, in German and Greek.

Continue along the north coast, hemming the sea. You will see the Rodopou Peninsula (Walks 12 and 13) lunging out ahead in the middle distance. Drive through **Tavronitis** (19.5km ✕⛽). **Kamisiana** (20.5km ✕) and **Rapaniana** (21km †▲ ✕⛽) flash by. On the far side of **Skoutelonas** (22km), look to the right, at the beginning of the peninsula, to see Moni Gonia (Walk 13). There is a wide three-way junction of roads at **Kolimbari** (where Walk 13 begins and ends). A turning right (signed to Afrata) goes into Kolimbari and to the Gonia Monastery — see them at leisure another day, or plan to do Walk 13.

Go sharp left at this junction, towards 'KISSAMOS', joining the A90 national highway after 1km, again heading west towards 'KISSAMOS'. After less than 4km you could turn off right for 'BEACH OF RAVDOUCHA' and then follow signs for 'RODOPOU' to get to Walk 12.
The main tour keeps to the A90. Soon, on the outskirts of Kissamos, the Gramvousa Peninsula is visible. The national highway passes through the centre of **Kastelli-Kissamos★** (Π▲✕⛽M). The town is certainly worth visiting; it

has a pleasant atmosphere. But we suggest you come another day, when you will have time to combine a visit with a walk or a swim at Falasarna's beach.

(*Detour:* As you drive through Kissamos, watch for a turn-off left to Polirinia at a junction with a central triangle, opposite a petrol station (37.5km ⛽). If and when

A good track extends almost to the end of the Gramvousa Peninsula, from where you can walk down to the bleached white sand fringing the turquoise lagoon of Balos (it's a stiff climb back up). Balos has become even more famous than the Samaria Gorge these days… and even more crowded; this photo was taken early in the morning.

you take this detour, you'll first pass a new church on the left and then continue inland, passing another sign for Polirinia at 39km. Go through Karfiana and Grigoriana before coming to Polirinia★ (44km ⛩✕). Drive to the end of the road and park near the taverna. Walk 14 ends here; if you'd like to stretch your legs, you could follow some of the walk in reverse, to the pleasant spot for Picnic 14 seen on page 10.)

Beyond the Polirinia turn-off you pass a small harbour and then the Kissamos port (41km) — from where boats offer day trips to Balos. The Gramvousa Peninsula spreads before you directly to the right, a brown-grey mound disappearing into the sea. At 47.5km a road (rough for the last kilometre) leads down right to Falasarna★ (⛩), where there is a good sandy beach — if you feel you have time for a swim. However, it will make your day very long to detour at this stage. If you decide to go for a swim, you could take the Elafonisi detour later in the day.

So keep up on the main road through **Platanos**, a long strung-out village. There's a good view back over the beach at 51km (📷); you can also see the tip of Falasarna. Then pass another good viewpoint

at 53km (📷), over the Bay of Sfinari. In **Sfinari** (58km ✕) we turn away from the sea and head up into the hills. The road passes through the tiny hamlet of **Ano Sfinari** (60km) and winds along beside a ravine, rounding its end at 62km. South of **Kambos** (66km) the road has recently been widened and rebuilt with barriers protecting the sheer drops to the sea. It used to be really unnerving — particularly between Kambos and **Keramoti**, a village that juts out off the hillside. **Amigdalokefali** is set mostly below the road, and then you pass through **Simadi** (77km), **Papadiana** (79km) and **Kefali** (81km ✕).

Half a kilometre beyond Kefali, turn right on a road signposted to 'ELAFONISI' and drive down through tree-covered hillsides to **Vathi** (83km). Go through pretty, white-washed **Plokamiana** and, after turning left round the Bay of Stomio, by 90km you can at last see the bright-white monastery ahead rising in the distance. An ugly rash of houses has sprung up at **Chrisoskalitisas** (91km ✕), just before the monastery★ itself (92km ✝).

Having visited the church, you're ready to start the return journey. But first, if you fancy a swim, take the route going right 0.5km past the monastery, signposted to Elafonisi. The lovely sandy beach with turquoise water is protected and created by the nearby Elafonisi Islands. Walk 19 can end at Elafonisi or the monastery.

Retracing the route from Chrisoskalitisas, turn right at 103.5km for 'HANIA'. Past **Louhi** (106km) fork right for 'ELOS'. **Elos** (108km ✕⛽) is a pretty village strung out amidst chestnut trees. Joining the Elos bypass road, turn right. Keep straight on at **Mili** (112km) and look out for any traffic coming in from the right (from Paleohora). Leave **Katsomatados** (Picnic 15; Walks 15 and 16) off to the right at 115.5km.

Soon you will have a wonderful view through the **Topolia Gorge★** (116.5km 📷). Just past this obvious viewpoint, there is a sign at the right of the road indicating the cave chapel of Agia Sophia★ (∩✝) up on the hillside at the left. Go through the narrow tunnel in the gorge wall (watching out for walkers!), then continue through the pretty hillside village of **Topolia** (118.5km), where Walk 16 ends, and **Voulgaro** (121.5km ⛽), where Walk 15 ends.

Reaching the old coast road at **Kaloudiana** (126km ✝), turn right for 'HANIA'. At **Koleni** (129km) turn left for 'NATIONAL ROAD'. Joining the A90 highway after 1km, make your way back to **Hania** (164km).

Moni Chrisoskalitisas (far left) and Elafonisi — before the crowds arrive

Car tour 2: PALEOHORA AND SOUTH COAST BEACHES

Hania • Tavronitis • Voukolies • Kandanos • Paleohora • Kandanos • (Sougia) • Hania

152km/94mi; 4 hours' driving; Exit B from Hania (town plan page 8). Roads are good, but those between Kandanos and Vlithias are very narrow and winding. Fill up with petrol before setting off, at Kandanos, or at Paleohora.

Walks en route: 1, 18, (19)

Picnic suggestions (see pages 10-13): (18 at Sougia)

You will see two coasts on this trip — the north coast, which you follow out of Hania, and the south coast at Paleohora, where there is a long beach stretching for miles east and west. The route cuts straight across the island from north to south as far as Kandanos, before descending torturously through Selinos (you will need a good map!) as you search out the district's many frescoed Byzantine churches. You might also like to make a detour to Anidri, where there is a church of particular interest.

Follow Car tour 1 as far as **Tavronitis** (19.5km). The turning you need in this village was not signposted at press date, so watch for the first zebra crossing and be prepared to turn left just metres past it — opposite the bus stop shaded by an attractive large tree. Pass through **Neranztia** (23.5km; ⛽ at 25.5km) and, in **Voukolies** (26km),

go through the main square. Then the main road heads right uphill, climbing out of this large village and the valley. Wind up through olive trees into the high hills. By about 33km you can see over the sea to the west coast on your right. Then, at **Dromonero** (34km), the countryside opens out, and you enjoy some very fine views.

Driving through the spread-out village of **Kakopetros** (38km), follow the road curving round to the right, towards 'PALEOHORA'. Catch your last glimpse of the north coast — with the Gramvousa Peninsula, shown on page 17, jutting out into the sea. The rockier landscape here is somewhat softened by horse chestnut trees. **Mesavlia** (43.5km) is just a few houses, followed by **Floria** (47km) and **Anavanos**. At

the end of the village of **Kandanos** (56km ✝⛽), follow the road round to the right. It then makes a wide arc to the left and heads south.

At **Plemeniana** (58km ✝) be sure to see Agios Georgios church with its 15th-century frescoes. It's not on the main road, but signposted off the right turn to Drys as you come into the village, past the Palios Mylios taverna. Some 2.5km further along the main road to Paleohora, just past a cement works on the right, turn off right for ΣΦΑΚΟΣ (Sfakos; only signed in Greek at time of writing). Go through Sfakos and 0.5km further on, turn left (not signed) at a T-junction to **Kakodiki** (63km ✝) to see the church of St Isidore and the frescoed chapel of Mikhail Arkhangelos (✝). Then continue

Above: eucalypts on the approach to Paleohora. Left: Psilos Volakas, about 1km west of Paleohora, is this tiny gem of a pebbly beach — one of the finest in Crete.

Left: lighthouse in Hania's Venetian harbour; below: on the Xiloskala

south, go through **Vlithias** (67km) and rejoin the main road. Soon the sea and the south coast come into view. Pass through **Kalamos** and **Ligia**, and then a rocky valley.

Paleohora (73.5km ▲△✕⛽) is approached along an avenue of eucalyptus trees. Just 0.5km further on, you pass the turn-off for Anidri★ (*not signposted* at time of writing). If you would like to see the 14th-century frescoes in Anidri's Agios Georgios church (✝), turn left just past the town hall (a tall building on the left, with flags) and just in front of a large yellow 'TAXI' sign. Then take the second left and carry straight on.

The main tour passes the Anidri turn-off and comes into Paleohora. Turn left at the 'STOP' sign and park on the sea-side esplanade. Walk 18, from Sougia via the site at Lisos, ends here, and Walk 19 to Elafonisi begins a taxi ride from here.

The simplest way to return to Hania is to retrace your outgoing route. But if you have decided to cover a lot of ground, it's possible to include Sougia in today's tour (add an extra hour and be sure to fill up with petrol). If you have a 4WD vehicle and can easily bump along unsurfaced roads, take the route via Anidri and Prodomi. Otherwise, drive northeast to Azogires and go via Strati and Temenia to Maza. From there follow the road through a gorge (📷) down towards the sea. When you meet the main Hania/ Sougia road, go right and start heading downhill to the coast. There's a good view of the towering wall of the White Mountains ahead of you as you descend. Drive through Moni and on to Sougia. To return from Sougia, pick up Car tour 3 at the 67km-point (page 25).

Car tour 3: COUNTRYSIDE, COASTAL BACKWATER AND HIGH CRETAN PASTURELAND

Hania • Nea Roumata • Agia Irini • Epanohori • Sougia • Omalos • Lakki • Fournes • Hania

159km/99mi; under 4 hours' driving; Exit B from Hania (plan page 8). Coming back down from Omalos you may well meet coaches — patience and care are required.

Walks en route: Walks 1, 2, 17, 18, 20-22

Picnic suggestions (see pages 10-13): 1 at Agia Lake, 17 at the Agia Irini Gorge, 17 at Sougia

This tour takes a very picturesque route through wooded valleys and the Agia Irini Gorge to Sougia, a pleasant backwater. En route one or some of your company might like to walk down the gorge (Walk 17) and meet up in Sougia. At Sougia, you may like to do the very attractive walk along another gorge to the site at Lisos, and then swim in the lovely clear water from Sougia's pebbly beach, before heading into the hills. The stretch to Omalos on the return journey is one of the most beautiful parts of the tour. So even if you're not going to 'walk Samaria', this tour will take you to the top — where shepherds gather on the plain and griffon vultures soar overhead.

'Taverna street' in Sougia

Leave Hania as for Car tour 1 on page 16 and bear left for 'NATIONAL HIGHWAY/OMALOS' at the wide Y-fork. Drive under the A90 highway and through the suburb of **Vamvakopoulo** (⛽), and then **Agia** (10km), setting for Walk 1 and a lovely place to picnic. Continue past a petrol station (⛽) and war memorial on the left, then bear right for 'SOUGIA' and 'SKINES' (12.5km). Cross the bridge over the Keritis River and, at the fork just past another petrol station and a supermarket, keep straight on (left). The road bypasses first Alikianos and then Skines. Once through **Hilaro** (20km) it won't be long before you are driving through wooded valleys, planted with citrus trees.

The road starts to climb seriously (22km) and becomes more twisty as it leads through the foothills of the White Mountains. Pass through **Nea Roumata** (29.5km) and **Prases** (30km ✝✕). Glorious hillsides surround you now — covered in chestnut, fig, olive, walnut and plane trees ... to name but a few. Pass the turning left for Omalos (38.5km), marked by wind turbines and various communication antennas.

Just beyond this turning, the Agia Irini Valley begins on the left; it runs through a gorge and down to the Libyan Sea, emerging at Sougia. Enter **Agia Irini** (42km). After you leave this village (a sign tells you so at 44km), watch for a board on the left announcing the Irini Gorge (Walk 17) — you may like to park there and enjoy a picnic in the pines.

Pass through **Epanohori**

(45.5km), from where you will have a first glimpse of the Libyan Sea, and start heading down to Sougia — via **Prines**, **Tsiskiana** and **Kambanos** (52km), beyond which the road swings round left and continues through **Maranes** and **Agriles** (56km). Turn left at the T-junction one kilometre past Agriles (Paleohora is off to the right — 22km away). In a kilometre or two you will have a splendid view over the valley and down to the sea, tucked neatly into the V ahead. **Moni** is the last village before **Sougia** (67km). Walk 17 ends in this backwater, and Walk 18 begins here. Our suggested picnic spot for Sougia, shown on page 101, is only 10-15 minutes away on foot.

After taking a break — perhaps on 'taverna street' — head back from Sougia the same way (via Moni, Agriles and Agia Irini). After 29km take the turning for Omalos passed earlier. Some 9km along, as you drive through a pass, the road goes by a small white church on the right. Now on the **Omalos** plain, keep right the next fork.

You reach the road which leads along the side of the plain to the top of the Samaria Gorge at a T-junction by the inviting-looking Agriorodo Villas. Bear right and drive to the **Xiloskala** at the top of the ravine. From here you can look down into the gorge itself (Walk 22) and up to Gingilos Mountain (Walk 20; photographs pages 105 and 110). You'll also see the route up to the mountain refuge at Kallergi, which we follow at the start of Walk 21. We hope this panorama will inspire you to walk!

From the Xiloskala keep on the main road back to Hania, about an hour's drive away. In pretty **Omalos** village (▲✕) you pass the Hotel Neos Omalos at the edge of the plain. Coach groups stop here for breakfast, en route for Samaria.

Leave the plain behind and start to descend towards the distant coast. The most noticeable place on the return route is **Lakki** (127km ✝✕), shown below. Take care past here to follow the road round to the right (132km) near the turning to Askordalos. Drive into **Fournes** (⛽), go over the bridge and curve left through the village. Pass the junction to Alikianos, and go straight on (⛽ 145km). After 8km you drive under the national highway and soon meet the turning right, back to the centre of **Hania** (159km).

View to Lakki

Car tour 4: THE AKROTIRI PENINSULA

Hania • Kounoupidiana • Stavros • Agia Triada • Moni Gouverneto • (Souda Bay Cemetery) • Hania

50km/31mi; 2 hours' driving; Exit C from Hania (plan page 8). Note: The Gouverneto Monastery is closed from 14.00-17.00, but the powers that be often close from 12.00. Dress appropriately: men should wear trousers and women longish skirts.

Walk en route: 11

Picnic suggestion (see pages 10-13): CT4 at Moni Gouverneto

The Akrotiri Peninsula, mushrooming out into the sea northeast of Hania, invites exploration. You may have seen some of it if you flew into Hania's airport, but you won't have seen any of the peninsula's treasures. The ruins of what is purported to be the island's earliest monastery are accessible by foot from this tour — as well as two other monasteries. All three are in lovely settings. With splendid views and swimming possibilities, this short tour could well fill a whole day very pleasantly.

Leave Hania by Exit C (El Venizelou): 1.5km from the market, follow the road round to the right, just beyond the Doma Hotel. The road, signed for the 'AIRPORT/ VENIZELOS' TOMBS', climbs up out of Hania, leaving the old part of town (Halepa) off to the left. The left turn you need to take to get out onto the peninsula comes up at 5km at a rather odd junction — a roundabout set off to the left: first go left for the 'VENIZELOS' TOMBS', then take the first right for 'STAVROS'. (But for a wonderful view of Hania, first detour *left* instead of right at this roundabout and drive for two minutes to the Venizelos' Graves, where you can gaze down over the town, the north coast, and Theodorou Island beyond (📷).)

Staying on the main route, very soon after the roundabout you will have another good view (📷) across Akrotiri to Stavros, where the mountain falls away into the sea. Coming to a large Y-fork at traffic lights (7km ⛽), take the right arm, then keep left and start heading downhill, through **Kounoupidiana** (✕). As you leave the village, turn sharp left at 8km for 'STAVROS'. **Kalathas Beach** (9km ✕) is passed, followed by **Horafakia**. On the edge of the latter, keep straight on for Stavros. Under 3km further on, turn right at a junction and come into **Stavros** (15km ✕); the lovely beach, shown above right, is perfect for swimming and picnicking.

Now head back the way you came, as far as the fork on the edge of **Horafakia**. Keep straight on here for Hania. At the next junction, some 300m further on, instead of going right, back to Hania, keep straight on (signposted 'AG TRIADA MONASTERY'). At the next fork (20.5km) go left (same signposting), heading towards the mast on the hill ahead. Three kilometres further on, at a 'STOP' sign, turn left (at time of writing there were signs ahead — one pointing in the direction you've come from Horafakia, the other right to Hania, but *no* sign pointing left). Drive down the avenue of trees to **Moni Agia Triada**★ (24km ✝✕).

After visiting the monastery, head on to Gouverneto, 4km away. With your back to Agia Triada, go

right. A sign for Gouverneto (ΓΟΥ–ΒΕΡΝΕΤΟ) takes you into a right turn at 25km. Apart from visiting **Moni Gouverneto**★ (29km ✝), why not picnic on the nearby slopes (Picnic CT4) or follow Walk 11 down to ancient Moni Katholikou, shown on pages 82-83?

Return to Agia Triada and, at the junction beyond the monastery (34km), go left for Hania. Just over 1km further on, turn right for 'HANIA'; the road curves round to the left, hemming the airport. Half a kilometre along, turn right; then turn right again at a roundabout (38km). Where the road divides at another roundabout (43km), either go left and down via the Souda Bay Cemetery and Souda or continue straight on to **Hania** (50km).

Top: Stavros, where the mountain falls into the sea and the beach is perfect for a swim and a picnic. 'Zorba the Greek' was filmed here. Middle: flower-bound house outside Hania. Bottom: children in regional costume at a remembrance service

Car tour 5: THE FOOTHILLS OF THE LEVKA ORI (THE WHITE MOUNTAINS)

Hania • Aptera • Katohori • Kambi • Mournies • Hania

67km/42mi; 2 hours' driving; Exit A from Hania (town plan page 8). Good roads throughout.
Walks en route: 3, 4

Picnic suggestions (see pages 10-13): 3 at Katohori or in the Diktamos Gorge, 4 just outside Kambi

History and hills combine nicely on this tour, which is a short spin into the lovely countryside inland from Hania. With the wild flowers of spring, the stillness of high summer or the colours of autumn, it's a pleasant morning or afternoon circuit. You'll drive to the fringe of the Levka Ori — often snow-capped until mid-summer.

Leave Hania by Exit A (Apokoronou; ⛽). At the traffic lights at the end of this avenue, go straight on for 'SOUDA/IRAKLION'. Then keep following signposting to Iráklion or Rethimnon, to eventually join the A90 national highway in the direction of Rethimnon and Iráklion.

Make the first move off the beaten track by turning right for 'APTERA' at 12km. At a junction after 1km (in an area called **Megala Horafia**, although it may not be signed as such) bear left at a brown sign for 'ANCIENT APTERA'. After one kilometre you will see **Aptera**★ (Π) spread out to the right. Drive on to the Turkish fort shown below; perched up in a commanding position, it looks out over another fort to Souda Bay (15km 📷).

From the fort go back to the junction in **Megala Horafia** and turn sharp left for Stilos, heading down through undulating hills. Make another sharp turn, this time to the right, at 20km ('MALAXA').

Beyond **Malaxa**, at 29km, turn left for Kambi and Kontopoula. (Turning *right* at this point, you would find a good taverna with magnificent views a minute away; ✗📷.) Head on to **Kontopoula** — a gorgeous panorama of hills and mountains is ahead.

At the Y-fork not far past Kontopoula, keep left into the next collection of houses on the route, **Katohori** (34km). At the far end of this village, turn left over the bridge (signpost: 'VOLIKAS SHELTER/ MADARO/KAMPOI'. Walk 3 starts here by the bridge, and you can park here to try either suggestion for Picnic 3 (there's a photo of the gorge on page 58).

Now make for **Kambi** (38km) and take the right-hand fork into the village square. The church and a *cafeneion* are on the right. Walk 4 is based here, and a 10-minute stroll along that route would take you to a lovely picnic setting.

Return the way you came; beyond the bridge at Katohori turn left instead of right. At the junction in **Gerolakos** (47km) turn right. Past **Loulos**, **Aletrouvari** and **Panagia** (where you pass a war memorial on the left), the route curves down the side of a steep valley, through **Vantes** and **Mournies** (62km). Now just keep ahead under the A90 national highway and then straight on in the one-way system to **Hania**'s market (67km).

From the Turkish hilltop fort above Aptera there are wonderful views. Most photos focus on the Turkish Itzedin fort just north of the A90 highway, with Souda Bay in the background. We pass it at the end of Car tour 6. The fort has had a chequered history: it was built by the Turks in the 19th century over Venetian ruins; it held political prisoners up until the 20th century, but today is in the hands of the navy and is sometimes used for cultural events.

Car tour 6: A SLICE OF CRETE

Hania • Vrises • Askyfou • Hora Sfakion • Frangokastello • Selia • Asomatos • Moni Preveli • Rethimnon • Georgioupoli • Hania

240km/149mi (via the old road from Rethimnon); 223km/138mi (via the A90 national highway from Rethimnon); 6-7 hours' driving; Exit A from Hania (town plan page 8). The road south, although it has undergone widening, is a mass of tortuous loops. Special care is needed when taking bends or overtaking (if you ever get the chance), because there are a lot of buses and coaches on this route. Fortunately their drivers are experienced! Note: Moni Preveli is open from 08.00-13.00 and from 15.00 to 18.00; dress appropriately: men should wear trousers and women longish skirts.

Walks en route: 2, 5, 6, (8, 9, 10), 25, 26, 27, 28

Picnic suggestions (see pages 10-13): 6 at Kournas Lake, (9a or 9b near Rethimnon, 10 in the Myli Gorge), 26 in the Imbros Gorge, 28 by the arched bridge over the Megalopotamos River, CT6 in the Kourtaliotiko Gorge

You'll sample a bit of everything on this tour, which encompasses a neat square of the island. First we head south, following the same route thousands of retreating, war-weary Antipodean and British soldiers trudged over during World War II. We call in at the pretty harbour village of Hora Sfakion, from where boats ply west to Loutro, Agia Roumeli at the foot of the Samaria Gorge, and Paleohora. We turn east, following the coast to Frangokastello, a solitary landmark, once a fortified castle. Past the Kotsifou Gorge, we visit one of Crete's most beautiful monasteries, Moni Preveli, set in glorious solitude. Heading north to Rethimnon, we leave the views over the Libyan Sea, following the Kourtaliotiko Gorge. Here it's really worth getting out of the car to walk down to a magical spot where there is a waterfall and a small church tucked away. From Rethimnon it's back to base — either via the old country road through Episkopi or along the direct A90 national highway.

Leave Hania by Exit A (Apokoronou; ⛽). At the traffic lights at the end of this avenue, go straight on for 'SOUDA/IRAKLION'. Then keep following signposting to Iráklion or Rethimnon, to eventually join the A90 national highway in the direction of Rethimnon and Iráklion. Pass the turning off to Aptera★ (12km; Car tour 5).

At 30km turn right towards 'VRISSES'. Turn left at the T-junction. After 1km, in **Vrises** (31km) you come to a three-way fork: take the middle route and head south ('SFAKIA', with the magnificent White Mountains rising to the right. Keep following 'SFAKIA', going left at a Y-fork after 750m (signed in Greek) and right at the following T-junction (not signed at all at time of writing). You soon pass the left turn to Alikampos (37km).

The road twists uphill, the landscape becoming rockier and greyer with the climb. There's a splendid sight as you round a corner (47km 📷): the plain of Askyfou, shown on page 132, spreads out across to the left of the road. A striking Turkish fort sits on a mound in the foreground. **Kares** (48km; Walk 27) is the little village on the hillock down to the left. The road hems the plain, and the next village is the main one of the area, **Askyfou** itself (49km ⛽). Drive on round the plain and then follow the road as it heads south again. This is the route that thousands of soldiers from Britain, Australia and New Zealand took when fleeing Western Crete.

The road skirts the Imbros Gorge, which you see down left at 55km. Walk 26 starts here; a shortish walk from **Imbros** would take you to the pretty picnic spot shown on page 129 — or there are pine-shaded picnic areas in the gorge itself (paid entry). Shortly (at 59km), if you look left again, you can see along the south coast to the east — including Frangokastello. But you are still high up above the sea and need to drive carefully as the road snakes its way down to the coast in loop after loop. At 68km, the coast road comes in from the east. Continue down and on into the pretty village shown on page 126, **Hora Sfakion★** (72km ⛰✕). As you curve down into the village, take the lower road to the harbour. Walks 22-26 finish at Hora Sfakion — by boat or on foot.

Head back out the way you came in and, at a Y-fork 3km uphill, bear right for 'FRAGO-KASTELLO' [sic], heading straight on along the coast. Pass through **Komitades** (76km); Walk 26 — which started out at Imbros — can end here at Komitades, or at Hora Sfakion. Continue on through **Vraskas**, **Vouvas**, **Nomikiana** and **Agios Nektarios** (where Walk 27 ends); then turn right at 83km for Frangokastello, heading down towards the sea.

After wandering round the ruined castle at **Frangokastello★** (87km Π; photograph overleaf), return to the main road and carry on, turning right to keep heading east. Drive through **Skaloti** and on to **Argoules**. Cross a stream and come into **Ano Rodakino** and **Kato Rodakino** (100km). Beyond the right-hand turn to Koraka Beach, the views are well worth stopping to admire. There is a particularly good viewpoint looking back west along the coast at 103km, and you can park at 104km to admire the panorama (📷✕): steep cliffs plunge down to the sea on your right, and the inland landscape is dramatically rocky and barren. A few kilometres further on you have views in all directions ... but nowhere to park.

The road bends down through **Selia** (111km). At 112km, take the sharp right turn downhill. It's the road from Rethimnon, skirting the Kotsifou Gorge; were you to turn left here, you would quickly come to the church shown on page 35. Walk 2 explores this gorge further south. From **Mirthios** (114km 📷✕) there

Mountains near Imbros

is a fine view over Plakias. Turn left at the roundabout where a sign points right to 'PLAKIAS 3KM' (115km). (But turn right here for Walk 2 or to swim or have a taverna lunch at Plakias Beach.) Then pass **Mariou**, set well up away from the sea; flat, cultivated land is on your right.

If you decide not to visit the Preveli Monastery (which would be a great pity), you will find Rethimnon signposted at **Asomatos** (122km ⛽). Here the main tour turns down sharp right into a bend; you will be heading almost back on yourself (there is a signpost here for the monastery and Plakias). After 1.5km turn left on a road which you will follow all the way to the monastery. To the left you see the Kourtaliotiko Gorge. Soon you pass the eye-catching arched bridge shown on pages 12-13; Walk 28 begins and ends here, and the surrounds are pleasant for picnicking. Keep going, past the ruins of the original 16th-century monastery★ (photo overleaf). Soon, just round a corner, over the hill, **Moni Preveli★** (129km ✝) comes into view. The setting, shown on page 134, is beautiful and very peaceful. Below the monastery the Megalopotamos River opens out into the sea at a palm-fringed beach (photo on page 137). Walk 28 is a superb circuit via Preveli.

The tour continues from Preveli by retracing the route past the original monastery and arched bridge to the main road (135km). Turn right, back to **Asomatos** (136km), then turn right again, for Rethimnon. This route takes you along the **Kourtaliotiko Gorge** for a short way. After 600m, you could pull into a parking bay (with a seasonal *kantina*), then walk ahead for 100m to a rock archway from where a path descends to the church of Agios Nikolaos and a splashing cool waterfall (Picnic CT6). Do make the effort to walk down — and back up. If you're lucky there won't be coachloads of other visitors.

From here head north. The countryside opens out at **Koxare** (143km). When you meet the main Rethimnon/Agia Galini road (144km), turn left (⛽ 151km). Pass a turning left to Hora Sfakion and continue into **Armeni** (157km ⛽). Before long the sea and the north coast are in sight in the distance and, as you approach Rethimnon, there is a very good view over the town and the New Harbour (📷). To explore **Rethimnon★** (167km **ΠΜ** ✕⛽⊕**M**) go under the national

Right: castle and beach at Frangokastello; below: Plakias beach (Walk 2)

highway and follow the road round, first to the left and then to the right, to park in the town centre (plan page 9). The old harbour is a good place to stretch your legs. More than any other town on Crete, this still speaks of its medieval past, with its Ottoman and Venetian buildings.

The museum houses a collection of coins and antiquities.

Leaving Rethimnon, make your way back onto the highway or, if you've still got some energy, follow us: go over the highway at large junction at the west end of Rethimnon, following the *blue* sign for 'ATSIPOPOULO' (171km). Heading south, you will drive through **Atsipopoulo**, **Prines**, **Gonia** and **Agios Andreas** in quick

succession — country villages set along a wooded valley. **Episkopi** (189km ⛽) is rather larger. Ignore a turning to Filaki; keep ahead and, in **Dramia** (193km), go sharp left (*not* signposted). Keep straight on when Filaki is indicated left again. There is a pretty church at the beginning of **Kournas** village (196km ✝📷), before you climb up through the village square. As you leave Kournas, you will see the north coast again, and then Crete's only natural freshwater lake will come into view below — the lovely, invigorating sight shown on pages 68-69 (198km; Walk 6), with several good picnic spots.

Pass the end of the lake and follow signs to Hania. Turn left for Hania at the T-junction (203km) and drive a short way alongside the national highway. The road then crosses over the highway, to come into the pretty main square of **Georgioupoli** (204km ⛰✕). Walk 5 makes a pleasing circuit from here to Selia and Exopolis (photo on page 65); Walk 6, another circuit, starts here, too, and visits Lake Kournas. Turn left at the Y-fork with a paved seating area in the middle, then go left again 150m further on.

This avenue of eucalyptus trees runs along at the right of the highway. Watch, after 5km, for where you can join the highway (*no* signposting at time of checking, but opposite the large Kanakis Olive Oil factory on the right). Turn right for Hania. You will pass the Turkish known as Itzedin — the focal point from Aptera shown on pages 28-29.

Left: Georgioupoli: a peaceful sight at the end of a rocky breakwater which protects the town beach to the right and the small harbour to the left (Walks 5 and 6). Right: St Nicholas church in the Kotsifou Gorge (top) and the ruins of the original Preveli Monastery south of Asomatos

Continue to **Hania** (240km). Leave the highway past the large 'Marakaki' building, where Hania and Souda are signposted in *green,* then turn left at the junction and go back to town the way you came out.

Car tour 7: CRETAN TREASURES

Hania • (Rethimnon) • Armeni • Spili • Agia Galini • Festos • Agia Triada • Hania

264km/164mi; about 6 hours' driving; Exit A from Hania (see town plan page 8). This tour follows major roads all the way.
Walk en route: (8, 9, 10), 30

Picnic suggestions (see pages 10-13): (9 near Rethimnon, 10 in the Myli Gorge; at the Minoan sites of Festos and Agia Triada

Well, this *is* a long haul, but it takes in a very large slice of Cretan landscape on the way to its goals, Festos and Agia Triada. We've included it because we are sure that many of you will want to make the effort to see two of Crete's major sites, even though you are based in Western Crete. To reach our destination, we travel via Spili — an exceedingly picturesque spot — and then between Mt Kedros and Siderotas.

Leave Hania by Exit A (Apokoronou; ⛽). At the traffic lights at the end of this avenue, go straight on for 'SOUDA/IRAKLION'. Then keep following signposting to Iráklion or Rethimnon, to eventually join the A90 national highway in the direction of Rethimnon and Iráklion. Pass the turning off to Aptera★ (12km; Car tour 5), Vrises

and Hora Sfakion (30km; Car tour 6), and Georgioupoli (33km; also Car tour 6). The road runs directly along by the sea from here to Rethimnon (⛽). You will have a good view of Rethimnon from the outskirts. Leave the highway at the exit for 'SPILI' (green board).

Head south now, through **Armeni** (70km ⛽ and nearby Minoan cemetery Π★), **Mixorouma** (86km ⛽; base for Walk 30) and **Spili** (89km ⌂✕), a large and pretty village well worth a 'pit stop'. Continue via **Kisou Kampos** (95km ⛽) and **Akoumia** (98km), where the road doubles back on itself briefly. Look up to Psiloritis — which is quite likely to be snow-capped until high summer. Take a moment, too, to admire the

Above: frescoes at Ag Georgios church in Mixorouma; left: Festos and the Mesara Plain

whole Ida range (📷), with Mt Kedros in the foreground.

Take the turning right to **Agia Galini** at 112km. The road divides: go left and drive down to the harbour of this busy resort (114km ⌂✕⛽). Then, having stretched your legs, head back to the main road. Keep ahead (right) at the junction, following signposting to Iraklion. At 122km you drive into the county of Iraklion, past a mass of plastic greenhouses, and then on via the ugly, functional spread of **Timbaki** (127km ⛽). The main road sweeps around to the right and before long you will see a sign indicating that Festos is 2km to the right.

The Minoan site of **Festos**★ (129km Π✕WC) is in a glorious position — with views towards the Dikti and Lasithi mountains to the

Agia Galini, against the backdrop of the Ida mountains. The village is a very popular tourist centre, so try to visit out of season.

east, the Ida range to the north, and the Asterousias to the south.

From Festos, carry on through the car park and fork right. This turning takes you back towards the Mesara Plain, to a spot from which you can walk down to **Agia Triada**★ (132km **Π**) in a few minutes. The remains of this Minoan summer palace are also in a delightful setting.

When it's time to head for home, simply retrace the route back to **Hania** (264km).

Car tour 8: THE AMARI VALLEY

Hania • Rethimnon • Apostoli • Thronos • Fourfouras • Agios ioannis • Gerakari • Rethimnon • Hania

240km/149mi; 6 hours' driving; Exit A from Hania (see plan page 8). The tour follows reasonable asphalted country roads, but they are narrow in places.
Walks en route: 7, (8, 9, 10) 29 (Walks 30, 31 and 32 are nearby)
Picnic suggestions (see pages 10-13): (9 in Rethimnon, 10 in the Myli Gorge), 29 near Ano Meros, Amari Valley (CT8)

The Amari Valley forms a natural route from the north to the south and so was much used as a refuge during the Second World War. Encircled by some forty villages and dotted with Byzantine churches, the valley offers up lovely countryside along our immediate route. But we also enjoy awe-inspiring, sweeping views encompassing the southwest slopes of Psiloritis, Crete's highest peak, and the string of mountains formed by Kedros, Soros, Fortetza and Vrissinas.

Follow Car tour 7 (page 36) to **Rethimnon**, but *pass* the turn off to Spili, which is taken in Car tour 7. Take the *next* exit, following signs for 'RETHIMNON' and 'AMARI', and then fork right for 'AMARI'. As you travel south, looking southwest, you will see Vrissinas, the highest peak across the valley (Walk 8). **Prasies** (71km ✝) is very pretty and shows signs of its Venetian past. Beyond the village, at the top of a ridge (72km), you enjoy the spectacular view (📷) towards the Prassanos Gorge shown on page 73. Soon, just past the right turn to Mirthios, you pass the starting point for Walk 7, which explores the gorge.

At a Y-fork before the **Potamon** (or **Amari**) **Dam**, go left ('FOURFOURAS', then 'VOLEONES'). The road edges the dam (📷). After hemming the northern side of the reservoir, turn sharp left for 'APOSTOLI'. **Apostoli** (90km ✝✕ and ⛽ just beyond the village) is at the head of the Amari Valley, and our circuit will bring you back to this point. Keep straight on through **Agia Fotini** (91km ⛽) and stay on the main road until, on a bend to the right, you see a sign for **Thronos**. It leads you left and up to the village (92km ✝). After visiting the 14th-century church of Panagia, return to the main road and turn left, continuing

Rethimnon's Venetian harbour

The Amari Valley

the circuit. Pass below Kalogeros (✝ with 14th-century frescoes), a pretty hillside village set up to the left of the road, and — a minute beyond here — look right to see the small 15th-century Byzantine church of Agia Paraskevi below you.

Pass the junction (93.5km) to Amari, following 'FOURFOURAS', and keep straight on the main road (⛽ 97km) as it curves left (where a right turn goes to Monastiraki). Go through **Afratas** (100km) and continue through groves of ancient olive trees, with fine views right towards Amari. Then come into **Visari** (103km). The road curls round the edge of the village and heads up to **Fourfouras** (105km ⛽), which is mainly set down to the right of the road. Behind Fourfouras lies Mt Kedros (1777m/5830ft) — a very comfortable mound, compared to the tantalising jagged teeth and high slopes of Psiloritis to the left of the road. Two kilometres past Fourfouras, as you continue to climb, look right and back over the village and the entire basin of the Amari Valley below you (📷).

Drive on via **Kouroutes** (112km ✝) and **Nithavris** (116km). Here, at the end of the village, turn right (by a war memorial) towards 'AGIOS IOANNIS'. This route cuts across the valley and goes through the upper part of **Agios ioannis** (120km). *Be sure to follow a hairpin bend round to the right* at 120.5km (*don't* go straight ahead for Agia Paraskevi). This bend now takes you through the lower part of Agios ioannis.

As you cross a bridge (125.5km) over the River Platys look right to see a picturesque old bridge (Picnic CT8). Past the bridge, the road starts to climb up the west side of the valley, above the olive tree line. Go through **Hordaki** (132km) in moments and **Ano Meros** (136km), where Walk 29 starts and ends. You could follow the first 20 minutes of that walk to a lovely picnic spot by a chapel (see page 38). There's a striking war memorial at the far end of Ano Meros, portraying a woman with a hammer in her hand.
Mt Samitos rises to the right of the small village of **Drigies** (138km). Move on through **Vrises** and **Kardaki** and then, just before Gerakari, keep watch on the right for the church of Agios Ioannis Theologos (✝), with 13th-century Byzantine frescoes. Even in autumn, **Gerakari** (145km) is visibly greener than the rest of the countryside. A cemetery on the left precedes **Meronas** (150km ✝), where fresh spring water pours down hillsides and where you turn right at the T-junction.

Turn left as you enter **Agia Fotini** (155km; *not* signposted) and go straight into **Apostoli**. You have now completed the valley circuit. Back in **Rethimnon**, join the A90 national highway and head west back to **Hania** (240km).

Walking

Western Crete is certainly a walkers' paradise but, even if you aren't an avid walker, there are plenty of opportunities for gentle strolls and rambles in the depths of the countryside, where you will develop a real appreciation for this magnificent corner of Greece. So if you can't 'do Samaria', you *could* manage a good number of our walks.

The 'Landscapes' series is built around walks and excursions that can be made *in day trips* from your home base. So all the walks in this book were originally conceived as day excursions *accessible by bus* from Hania or Rethimnon. These days many people are keen to hire cars and would prefer circular walks. But the beautiful old donkey trails and mountain paths were built to take people and livestock from one place to another: they are all linear. One solution is to just walk part-way and return to your car. Another solution —where possible — is to walk from A to B and take a bus back to your car (or, to be on the safe side, drive to the end of the walk, leave your car there, and take a bus back to the start). Suitable walks (not necessarily circular) are indicated by a symbol in the Contents. It may be one of the *variations* of the main walk that is recommended: look for the symbol under 'Access' (with waypoints for the walk start so that you can set your satnav).

Do consider combining some of the walks by spending a night or two away from your hotel, thus making a patchwork of mountain, gorge and coastal paths (see Walks 17-27 for instance). Just a word of caution: ***never try to get from one walk to another on uncharted terrain!*** Only link up walks by following paths described in these notes, shown on good maps, or by using roads or tracks; don't try to cross rough country (which might be dangerous) or private land (where you might not have the right of way).

The people you meet are very much a part of the landscape, countryside and essence of Crete. Do greet anyone you pass or see working in a field when you are out walking. Please don't — perhaps through your natural reserve — pretend they don't exist!

There are walks in this book for everyone.

Beginners: Start on the walks graded ● or ●, and check all the short and alternative walks. The picnic suggestions on pages 10-13 offer a large selection of very easy walks.

Experienced walkers: If you are accustomed to rough

terrain and are feeling fit, you should be able to enjoy all our walks. Many — especially those in gorges — require agility, and a couple will demand a head for heights as well. Take into account the season and weather conditions: don't attempt the more strenuous walks in high summer; protect yourself from the sun and carry ample water.

Experts: Head for the high mountains. Both the White Mountains and the Ida Range (Psiloritis) will be a great attraction for you (Walks 4, 20, 21, 31).

Grading, waymarking, maps, GPS

We've tried to give you a quick overview of each walk's **grade** in the Contents. But many of our walks have shorter or alternative versions! In the Contents we've only had space to show the *lowest* grade of a *main* walk: for full details, including easier versions, see the walk itself. Here is a brief overview of the four gradings:

● very easy — more or less level (perhaps with a short climb to a viewpoint); good surfaces underfoot; easily followed

● easy-moderate — ascents/descents of no more than about 300-500m/1000-1800ft; good surfaces underfoot; easily followed

● moderate-strenuous — ascents/descents may be over 500m/1800ft; variable surfaces underfoot — you must be sure-footed and agile; possible route-finding problems in poor visibility

● expert — only suitable for very experienced hillwalkers with a head for heights; hazards may include landslides or balancing on ledges with no respite from constant exposure

Any of the above grades may be followed by:

❢ *danger* of vertigo; the walk demands a good head for heights

Assigning grades to walks is *very* subjective — and giving them a 'vertigo' rating even more so! Until you get used to Crete's terrain and know your 'vertigo tolerance', why not try walking with one of the many **guided groups**? Note also: should you wish to walk further afield, we suggest you contact the Alpine Club in Hania (www.eoshanion.gr; see plan on page 8) or the refuge at Kallergi (see the 'Short walk' on page 108 and the photos on pages 109 and 110).

It's always encouraging to see **waymarking** along the route. But, unless we specifically advise you to follow it, don't *rely* on waymarking. You will certainly be following parts of the 'E4' network of long-distance routes. These 'European Rambler Trails' are usually well waymarked with yellow paint and signposted with yellow and black triangular plaques. If a walk in this book has become part of the E4, we mention this and

Right: a cool leafy glade — this is the church of Agios Antonios, where Walk 9 nears its end, just above Myli.

show the route on the walking map — but the E4 is growing all the time, so we may be a bit out of date! (The entire **E4 trail across Crete** is shown on our touring maps, but there is a wealth of helpful information on the web.)

The **maps** in this book are based on Openstreetmap mapping (see page 2), but have been very heavily annotated from our notes and GPS work in the field. We hope that these maps, which we have found to be *very* accurate on the ground, will be a boon to walkers. It is a pity that we have to reproduce them at only 1:50,000 to keep the book to a manageable size; quite a few walkers buy both the paperback *and* download our pdf files so that they can enlarge the maps — or you can enlarge them on a colour photocopier. Otherwise, we recommend the widely available GPS-compatible Anavasi 1:25,000 maps.

Free **GPS track** downloads are available for all our walks: see the Western Crete page on the Sunflower website. Please bear in mind, however, that GPS readings should *never* be relied upon as your sole reference point, as conditions can change overnight. *But even if you don't use GPS,* our maps are now so accurate that you can easily compare them with Google Maps on your smartphone and pinpoint your exact position. And it's great fun opening out GPS files in Google Earth to preview the walks in advance!

Things that bite or sting

Dogs on Crete, in our experience, are full of bravado, but not vicious. They bark like fury — indeed, what would be the point of guarding livestock if they did not? — and they will approach you, seemingly full of evil intention. However, they will shy off if you continue unperturbed. '**El**-la' is a useful word to know. It means 'come here', if spoken encouragingly, or 'come off it', when said in a slightly diffident tone. Use it encouragingly with the dogs, and they'll soon go away. If you carry a walking stick, keep it out of sight and don't use it threateningly. If dogs worry you, you may like to invest in a 'Dog Dazer' — an ultra-sonic device which deters threatening dogs without harming them. These are widely available on the web.

In the autumn you may be startled by gunfire, but it's only **hunters** — invariably on Sundays and holidays — in pursuit of game. You'll doubtless see them dropping or throwing stones into bushes — Greek beating!

Snakes may be seen, and vipers have been identified on Crete, but they keep a very low profile and are not widespread. Poisonous **spiders**, called 'rogalida', do exist on the island, but it's highly unlikely you'll even catch a glimpse of one, as they are

On the E4 trail to Lisos (Walk 18): the familiar yellow sign on a tree (background, left) and one of the 'poached egg' waymarks on a boulder in the foreground

burrowers. You're more likely to see **scorpions**; they are harmless, but their sting is painful. Like spiders and snakes, they are likely to be hiding under rocks and logs in the daytime hours. So if you move a rock, etc, to sit down, just have a look under it first.

Have respect for **donkeys**' hind legs; it's highly unlikely they'll kick, but don't forget the possibility.

People who are allergic to bee stings should always carry their medication. **Bees** abound in high summer, especially around water troughs and thyme bushes.

Although we've mentioned this collection of creatures, it's very doubtful indeed that you will encounter anything that would harm you.

What to take

If you're already on Crete when you find this book, and you haven't any special equipment such as a day rucksack or walking boots, you can still do many of the walks — or you can buy the basic equipment at one of the sports shops in Hania or Rethimnon. Don't attempt the more difficult walks without the proper gear. For each walk in the book, the *minimum* equipment is listed. Above all, you need thick-soled stout walking trainers or walking boots. *Ankle support* is advisable in your footwear — indeed *essential* on many of the walks, where the path descends steeply over loose stones. You may find the checklist on the next page useful:

- walking trainers or walking boots
- long trousers, tight at the ankles
- long-sleeved shirt (sun protection)
- waterproof rain gear
- telescopic walking stick(s)
- mobile phone (**112 is the Europe-wide emergency number**)
- water bottle, plastic plates, etc
- tissues
- sunhat, sunglasses, sun cream
- groundsheet
- up-to-date bus timetable
- windproof (zip opening)
- bandages and plasters
- extra pair of (long) socks
- knives and openers
- light jerseys (or similar)
- antiseptic cream
- whistle, torch, compass/gps
- spare bootlaces
- small rucksack
- insect repellent

Please bear in mind that we've not done *every* walk in this book under *all* conditions. We might not realise, for example, just how hot or how exposed some walks might be. Beware of the sun and the effects of dehydration. Don't be deceived by cloud cover: you can still get sunburnt, especially on the back of your neck and legs. We rely on your good judgement to modify the 'equipment' list at the start of each walk according to the season.

Where to stay

We have used Hania as our walking base, since the majority of people stay there when visiting Western Crete. But we have taken into account those of you staying at Rethimnon, Kastelli-Kissamos, or along the south coast, and you will find that you can join many of the car tours without difficulty. Several walks will be on your doorstep, but check the bus timetables (pages 149-150) to make sure that those furthest from your base are practicable. Due to the size of the island, some of the walks require bus changes. Although this makes the day longer, it has the advantage that you see more of the countryside. To find rooms in small villages, enquire at the local tavernas and *cafeneions* about renting a bed for a night. An overnight stay at the comfortable, staffed mountain refuge at Kallergi (see page 108) is recommended for those of you wanting to experience the Levka Ori — or you could stay down on the Omalos plain.

Walkers' checklist

The following points cannot be stressed too often:

- **At any time a walk may become unsafe** due to storm damage or bulldozing. If the route is not as described in this book, and your way ahead is not secure, do not attempt to continue.
- **Never walk alone** — four is the best walking group.
- **Transport** connections at the end of a walk are vital.
- Proper **footwear** is essential.

- **Warm clothing** is needed in the mountains; even in summer, take something appropriate with you, in case you are delayed.
- **Mobile/smartphone, compass/gps, torch, whistle** weigh little, but might save your life.
- **Extra food** and drink should be taken on long walks.
- Always take a **sunhat** with you, and in summer a cover-up for your arms and legs as well.
- A **stout stick** or **telescopic walking pole** is a help on rough terrain and to discourage the rare unfriendly dog.
- Read and reread the **important note** on page 2 and the Country code on page 11, as well as guidelines on grade and equipment for each walk you plan to do.

Weather

April, May, September and October are perhaps the best months to walk on Crete. The air temperature is moderate, but the sun shines. It is possible to walk during June, July and August, however, because although it may be very hot by the coast, there's often a light breeze in the mountains. There's no doubt it's more tiring though, and great care should be taken in the sun and heat. Walks offering little or no shade (for instance Walks 12 on the Rodopou Peninsula) should only be undertaken in high summer *with great caution*.

The *meltemi* blowing in from the north tends to be a bad-tempered wind, bringing strong, hot breezes in the height of summer. These breezes stir up the dust, move the air about, but don't really cool it.

During February and November it often rains. The months of December and January are chilly and, if it rains, it may do so for two or three days at a time. However, the winter in Crete brings an incredible clarity on sunny days and some really perfect walking weather, when temperatures may be around 20°C (68°F).

It's worth remarking, too, that more often than not, when it's windy along the north coast, it's calm on the south of the island.

Greek for walkers

In the major tourist areas you hardly need to know any Greek but, once you are out in the countryside, a few words of the language will be helpful. Anyhow, it's nice to try to communicate — if only a little — and people will marvel at your attempts.

Here's one way to ask directions in Greek *and understand the answers you get!* First memorise the few 'key' questions given below. Then, always follow up your key question with a **second**

question demanding a yes (ne) or no (ochi) answer. (By the way, Greeks invariably raise their heads to say 'no', which looks to us like the beginning of a 'yes'. And 'ochi' (no) might be pronounced as **o**-hee, **o**-shee or even **oi**-ee.)

Following are the two most likely situations in which you may have to use some Greek. The dots (...) show where you will fill in the name of your destination. The approximate pronunciation of place names is in the Index.

▪ Asking the way

The key questions

English	*Approximate Greek pronunciation*
Good day, greetings (formal)	**Hair**-i-tay
Hello, hi (informal)	**Yas**-sas (plural); **Yia**-soo (singular)
Good morning/afternoon	Kah-lee-**may**-rah/Kah-lee-**spay**-rah
Please —	**Sas** pa-ra-ka-**loh** —
where is	**pou ee**-nay
the road that goes to ... ?	o **thro**-mo stoh ... ?
the footpath that goes to ... ?	ee mo-no-**pa**-ti stoh ... ?
the bus stop?	ee **sta**-ssis?
Many thanks.	Eff-hah-ree-**stoh** po-**li**.

Secondary question leading to a yes/no answer

English	*Approximate Greek pronunciation*
Is it here?	**Ee**-nay **etho**?
Is it there?	**Ee**-nay eh-**kee**?
Is it straight ahead?	**Ee**-nay kat-eff-**thia**?
Is it behind?	**Ee**-nay **pee**-so?
Is it to the right?	**Ee**-nay thex-**ya**?
Is it to the left?	**Ee**-nay aris-teh-**rah**?
Is it above?	**Ee**-nay eh-**pano**?
Is it below?	**Ee**-nay **kah**-to?

▪ Asking a taxi driver to take you somewhere and return for you, or asking him to collect you somewhere

English	*Approximate Greek pronunciation*
Please —	**Sas** pa-ra-ka-**loh** —
would you take us to ... ?	tha **pah**-reh mas stoh ... ?
Come and pick us up	**El**-la na mas **pah**-reh-teh
from ... (place) at ... (time)*	apo ... stees ...*

**Instead of memorising the hours of the day, simply point out on your watch the time you wish to be collected.*

As you may need a taxi for some walks, why not ask your tour rep or hotel reception to find a driver who speaks English (many now do). We'd also recommend an inexpensive phrase book with easily-understood pronunciation hints, as well as a good selection of useful phrases.

By the way: it's unlikely that a map will mean anything to the *older* people you may meet en route. Doubtless, they will ask you '**Pooh pah**-tay?' — at the same time turning a hand over in the air, questioningly. It means 'Where are you going?', and quite a good answer is 'Stah voo-**na**', which means 'to the mountains'.

Organisation of the walks

The 32 main walks in this book are located in the parts of Western Crete most easily accessible by public transport, using Hania (or Rethimnon) as the base. We hope that even if you're staying somewhere else in the west, most will be within range — especially if you've hired a car. (Although the walking notes show bus departures from Hania, you will find more complete timetables on pages 149-150, including Rethimnon, Kastelli-Kissamos, etc.)

The book is set out so that you can plan walks easily — depending on how far you want to go, your abilities and equipment — and what time you are willing to get up in the morning! You might begin by considering the fold-out touring map inside the back cover of the book. Here you can see at a glance the overall terrain, the road network, and the general location of the walks. Quickly flipping through the book, you'll find that there's at least one photograph for each walk.

Having selected one or two potential excursions from the map and the photographs, look over the planning information at the beginning of each walk description. Here you'll find distance/hours, grade, equipment, and access. If the walk sounds beyond your ability or fitness, check to see if there's a shorter or alternative version. We've tried to provide walking opportunities less demanding of agility wherever possible.

When you are on your walk, you will find that the text begins with a general introduction and then quickly turns to a detailed description of the route itself. As well as distances, *times* are given for reaching certain points in the walk. Once you've done one walk, you'll be able to compare our very steady pace with your own; we hope you'll find we're in step, give or take! *Note that our times do not include any stops, so do allow for them.*

Below is a key to the symbols used on our large-scale walking maps.

Walk 1: CIRCUIT VIA AGIA

Church at Stalos

Distance: 13.2km/8.2mi; 3h15min
Grade: ● straightforward walk on asphalt roads, with about 200m/650ft of ascents overall
Equipment: trainers, sunhat, picnic, water
Picnic: at Lake Agia
Access: any blue city 🚌 calling at Kato Stalos (not in the Timetables, but every 5-10 minutes); journey time 10min

Shorter walk: Kato Stalos to Agia (7km/4.3mi; 2h10min). ● Grade, equipment, access as above. Follow the main walk to Agia; return to Hania by Omalos 🚌 (Timetable 3), Sougia 🚌 (Timetable 6), or blue town 🚌.

Short walk: Agia — Lake Agia — Agia (2km/1.2mi; 35min). ● Easy, level walk. Access: 🚗 or Omalos 🚌 (Timetable 3), Sougia 🚌 (Timetable 6), or blue town 🚌 to the Agia bus stop on the main road. Then walk east to the turning 'LAKE OF AGYIA' and turn left. Pass Agia church on the left (where motorists can park: 35° 28.509'N, 23° 55.812'E). Then turn right to the lake. Return the same way. ()

Alternative walk: Agia to Platanias (7.5km/4.7mi; 2h). ● Easy, mostly level walking; access as *Short walk;* equipment/return as main walk. Follow the *Short walk* to the lake, then walk on to **Kirtomados** and pick up the main walk at the 2h-point, passing the CHURCH on your right.

Since we first walked here, much has been done to improve the lake at Agia as a recreational area (the new bridge shown overleaf is an example), but so far it has escaped the more commercialised fate of Lake Kournas (Walk 6). Agia's lake (actually a man-made reservoir) is a particularly good place to watch birds, a lovely quiet oasis overlooked by the church of Saints Constandinos and Eleni — hence the name Agia ('holy'). This walk is all along asphalt country roads, but it is a welcome respite from the urbanisation around the coast, and the views to the Levka Ori (White Mountains) are stunning.

Start out at **Kato Stalos** (●): take the road opposite the Tropicana Beach Resort (which *should* be signposted to STALOS). When it forks (**10min**; the national highway is visible up ahead) go left uphill, passing under the highway. At the fork just past the highway, turn right towards PANO STALOS and follow the road across a small valley. Within a couple of minutes (**15min**) you will see on the left, across the valley, a lovely old house called **Metochi** (ⓐ). It is a classic example of the

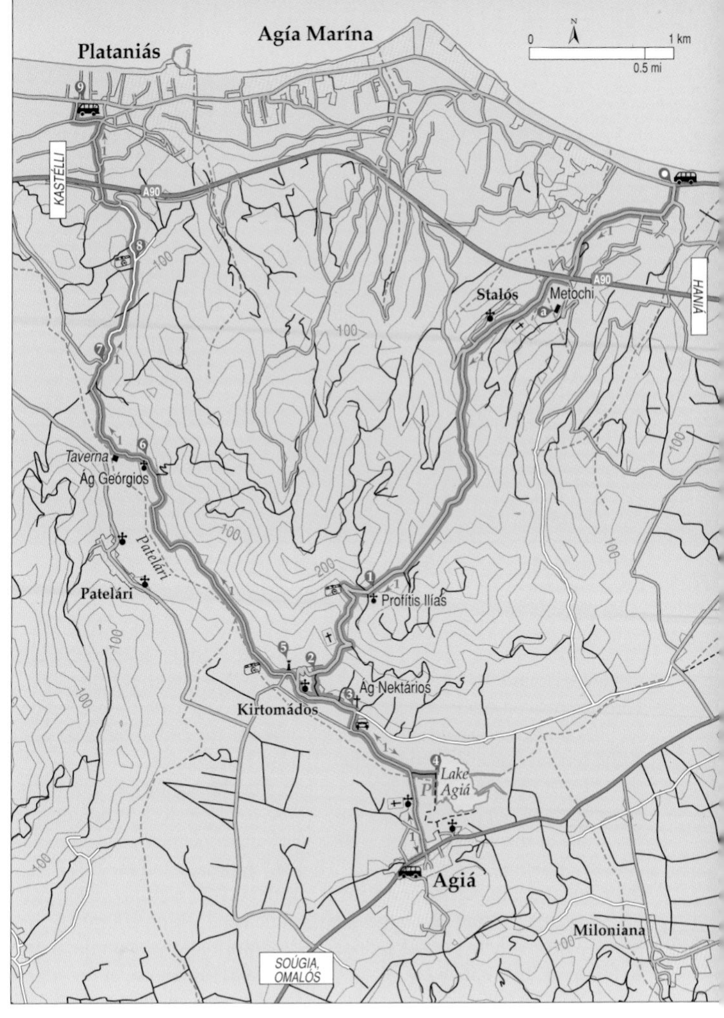

Turkish style of the 1700s. To its right, beyond its garden, under two or three large trees, you may see a semi-circular hole in the wall. Water from the mountains, flowed through this hole into a stone pool. The water, having been used for washing clothes and people, was then drained into the valley to water the fruit trees.

Beyond a CEMETERY, keep up into the old village of **Stalos**, passing a few tavernas. In the village centre, opposite a *cafeneion*, continue straight ahead (a right turn would lead to the church shown opposite). Bear left at the next Y-fork, leaving Stalos on a wide asphalted road, through olive groves. Ignore all turnings.

The road climbs gently away from the coast, levels out, then starts to descend. You pass the small church of **Profitis Ilias** up to the left (❶); almost hidden by trees; **1h**). There is a fine panorama of countryside ahead as you continue along the road. Soon you may spot a church and graveyard below.

Before long you will see your destination down and across to your left. First of all a church comes into

For Picnic 1 you can either find a quiet corner of the lake at Agia or sit by this attractive modern bridge

view; then you'll see the lake in the distance. Round the next bend, Kirtomados comes into range. Pass the first house in **Kirtomados** and, at the second house (on your right), take a CONCRETE TRACK (❷) left downhill between more houses. In the midst of the village, weave right and, at a junction of sorts (where there's a large mulberry tree on the left), turn left in front of a large old house with an arched wooden door. In 50m/yds, by a shady taverna on the right, turn left on the road. At the next JUNCTION (❸), where there is a small shrine dedicated to **Agios Nektarios** off to the left of the signposts, follow the road round to the right.

Some **1h45min** en route, just before a bridge, take a track going left. In two minutes you will be at the edge of the LAKE (❹). This is a very pretty place to picnic, but there is also a tastefully-finished 'bird-watchers' café'. Look out for terrapins, too, basking on the rocks in summer.

If you are doing the Shorter walk, from here head back to the road, go left and continue to the main Hania road at **Agia**; both the blue city buses and the country buses stop opposite the end of this road coming from Kirtomados.

For the main walk, return the way you came to **Kirtomados** (**2h**). Pass the concrete track you took on your approach and the CHURCH, both on your right. Fork left past the church and within 100m/yds pass a WAR MEMORIAL (❺) on the right. Just 30m further on, at the edge of the village, turn right towards PLATANIAS (signposted in Greek, Πλατανιασ; straight on is signposted to Patelari.) There is a lovely view to the White Mountains on the left. Now just stay on this country road, ignoring any turnings.

The road starts to rise and you glimpse the **Patelari River** down to the left, through the trees. Five minutes later Patelari's two distinctive churches come into view on the left, across an orange grove. The road bends to the left and then right, and you can enjoy two to three minutes of plane tree-shade, with orange groves on the right. It is

Quiet corner by the lake in Agia

hard to believe that the hubbub of the coastal villages is so near.

Some 30 minutes from Kirtomados (**2h30min**) you pass the tiny church of **Ag Georgios** (⑥) — known locally as 'Drunk George', almost hidden in bougainvillaea. It's usually locked. Then, five minutes later, you arrive at the lovely DRAKIANA RIVERSIDE RESTAURANT on the left — a gloriously shady riverside taverna, a perfect place for a leisurely pit stop.

Having relaxed and eaten some delicious home-cooked food, continue on the road. Ten minutes from the taverna (where the road curves left and there is a mass of water pipes on the right), leave the road: go straight ahead on a ROUGHISH TRACK (⑦), the surface of which varies. Ignoring a minor crossing track and then a track to the left, follow this main track to the top of the hill, where the sea comes into view. Then, at a Y-fork, head left downhill (⑧). Ignore another fork off left, join an asphalt road after 350m/yds and follow it to the left. Just 100m further on turn off right, to walk under the national highway. Then walk straight ahead past PLATANIAS PARK and the large PRIMARY SCHOOL. When the road divides 200m past the school, curve round to the left. A minute later, turn right; after 100m/yds you will meet the main coast road in **Platanias**. Turn right; the BUS STOP (⑨; **3h15min**) is on your right.

See also photo on pages 32-33
Distance: 6km/3.7mi; 3-4h
Grade: ● adventurous, but suitable for anyone who is sure-footed and doesn't mind wading in *waist-deep* water at times (be prepared to get dirty, too). Ascent/descent about 200m/650ft overall. Not suitable after heavy rain
Equipment: bathing things and wading shoes, waterproof bag for camera, dry clothes/shoes, sunhat, picnic, water
Picnic: anywhere in the gorge
Access: 🚗 to/from Plakias (park at the seafront by the bus stop: (35° 11.423'N, 24° 23.714'E), or 🚌 from Rethimnon (Timetable 15); journey time 40min

Short walks

1 *The 'Old Mill' and Mirthios* (4.7km/3mi; 1h45min). ● Easy walk on tracks and paths, with about 200m/650ft of ascent. The stepping stones may prove difficult after rain. Trainers, sunhat, picnic, water. Access as main walk. Follow the main walk to the 'OLD MILL' (❻; **40min**), then take the signposted path to Mirthios — at first following the line of the aqueduct. After the path makes a U-turn to the right there's a nice view down to the tiny chapel visited earlier. Then the path merges with a track, from where Plakias is visible down on the coast. Continue in the same direction. (If you see any offshoot to the left after about 50m, ignore it and keep right.) Contouring below a house, you come to a concreted T-junction, where you turn left, steeply uphill. At the next T-junction turn right to the old village WASHHOUSE in **Mirthios**. Just past it, take wide stone steps up past TAVERNA VRISI to the main village street and BUS STOP (❼; **1h15min**). After looking around and having some refreshment — perhaps in TAVERNA PLATEIA, with its stunning views, head back to the WASHHOUSE and turn left, then immediately right. Follow this little-trafficked road all the way down to the BUS STOP in **Plakias** (**1h45min**).

2 *Old Mill* (3.3km/2mi; 1h15min). ● Equipment/access/ grade as Short walk 1, but only 50m/165ft of ascent. Follow the main walk to the 'OLD MILL' (❻; **40min**), then retrace steps to where you crossed on STEPPING STONES (❸). Keep straight on here, ignoring all turnings to the right, all the way back into **Plakias** (**1h15min**).

The popular walk to the 'Old Mill' above Plakias can be extended to make a real adventure. From the mill we continue upstream in the Kotsifou Gorge. There's no path, so much of the time you will be *in* the stream itself.

Start the walk at the BUS STOP (○) in the centre of **Plakias**: follow the coastal road west towards the pier, crossing a BRIDGE over the mouth of the **Kotsifou Stream**. Take the next, narrow street to the right. At the junction after 250m/yds, turn hard right (signed to the youth hostel), recrossing the stream on another BRIDGE. The road bends left and passes the YOUTH HOSTEL (❶) and then a LIBRARY run by British ex-pats (who are a great source of local information). By now there's gravel underfoot.

Keep straight on. Just over 500m past the library you come to a first old MILL(❷). (There are three

Right: the 'Old Mill' above Plakias

16th-century Venetian mills in the gorge; we visit all three on the main walk; the other versions visit only two.) This one has mostly collapsed, but parts of its impressive aqueduct remain. The village of Mirthios is visible up to the right from here.

Just under 100m past the mill turn left at a fork; then, 100m further on, go left at a Y-fork. Go left at the next fork, too, on a path down to a tiny field and then the stream. (This path moves from year to year; if it's overgrown, there is another path 100m further along, just before a stock control gate.) Cross the stream on STEPPING STONES (3) — tricky after heavy rain. On the far side, turn right on a track which narrows to a path. Carry straight on past an ARCHED BRIDGE (4) on the right — to a tiny whitewashed CHAPEL (5), partially built into the rock. There's a good view from here to the sea.

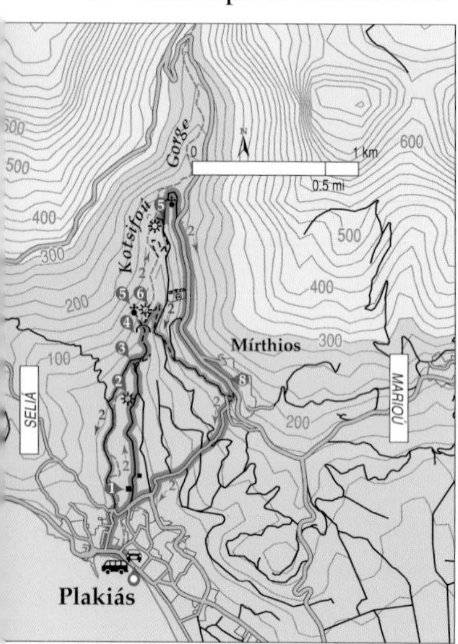

Return the 50m to the BRIDGE (❹) and cross it, then climb up to the second MILL — known as 'THE OLD MILL' (❻; **40min**). This is a very substantial affair — you can see its walls rising above the vegetation. If you climb up and wander around the aqueduct, taking in the mill's layout, you may realise that this mill had a double function: water from the permanently flowing stream powered the grain-grinding apparatus on the upper floor, while the overflow water was used to wash wool or handwoven fabrics below.

Now walk back to the arched bridge (❹), cross it and turn right. *(Short walk 2 goes left here.)* Make your way down into the stream. Now the fun begins. Depending on the time of year and seasonal rains, you may get *very* wet as you head upstream, wading and clambering over rocks and boulders, sometimes dodging waterfalls, sometimes luxuriating in these 'power showers', sometimes bathing in the pools.

After 5-600 metres you come to a crumbled road by a third ruined mill. Walk ahead to where this road has been overlaid with newer concrete, and follow the concrete round to the right — to another bit of crumbled road/track, where you make a U-turn to the left. This rounds a chapel to the main road, which you follow downhill. There is no pavement, but there is room to get off the road should a car appear.

After taking a break at **Mirthios** (❼; **2h30-3h30min**) — perhaps in *TAVERNA PLATEIA*, with its stunning views — walk a few metres further on, to the small parking area/BUS STOP. Then, opposite a gift shop, take broad steps down (past *TAVERNA VRISI* on the left) to the road. Turn left, then turn right immediately.

On the descent a conical hill crowned by the remains of Plakias Castle can be glimpsed off to the east. All that is left of this Venetian fortress are the yellowish chapel walls. (During the Second World War, the Germans also appreciated the strategic significance of the bay, and the cliffs to the east are honey-combed with tunnels and gun turrets.) Back in **Plakias**, retrace steps to the BUS STOP (**O**; **3-4h**).

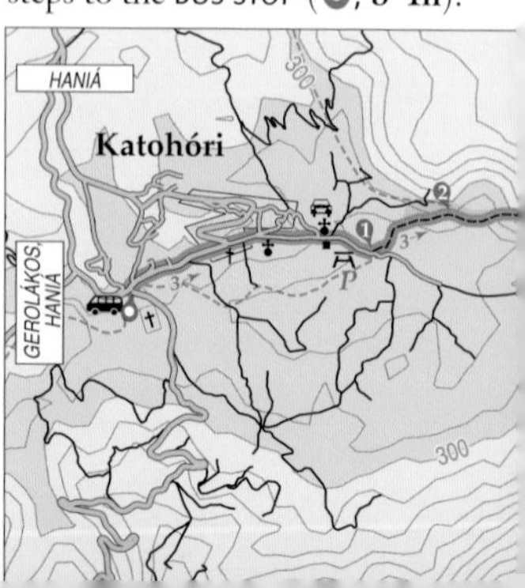

Walk 3: THE DIKTAMOS GORGE: FROM KATOHORI TO STILOS (OR NIO HORIO)

Distance: 9km/5.6mi; 3h35min to Stilos (10.4km/6.4mi; 4h to Nio Horio)
Grade: ● moderate-tough; way-marked gorge walk descending 250m/820ft; much clambering over boulders necessary
Equipment: walking trainers or boots, sunhat, picnic, water
Picnic: at the start of the walk or in the gorge
Access: Kambi 🚌 to Katohori (not in the timetables; departs Hania 14.00 Mon/Wed/Fri only); journey time 35min. Return on 🚌 from Stilos (not in the timetables; departs 16.45 in season; enquire locally); journey time 30min. Or 🚌 from Nio Horio (not in the timetables; departs 11.15, 13.10, 17.30 weekdays, 11.15, 16.20, 18.30 Saturdays/Sundays in season; enquire locally); journey time 30min. If travelling by 🚗, see Picnic 3 on page 11 to park in Kambi, visit the gorge, and return the same way.

This is a very pleasant, but somewhat taxing walk through a glorious gorge. The bus ride from Hania is well worth the early start. The White Mountains rise in an awesome but splendid mass to one side as you climb into the foothills. The gorge is an attractive walking route, fringed with leafy plane trees and hemmed with pretty pink oleander bushes. The walk is demanding in many places, as the gorge floor offers every kind of surface underfoot. If you encounter any stock control gates, please re-fasten them after passing through.

The bus stops at a junction just before a BRIDGE (O) on the south side of **Katohori**, where a road heads south (signposted to Madaro and Kambi). **To start the walk,** head east along the road signposted 'DIKTAMOS GORGE' (among others). The river bed that runs through the gorge to Stilos is down to your right. On the first big U bend to the left (sign: 'DIKTAMOS GORGE'), where there is a MINIATURE CONCRETE CHURCH, leave the main road and carry straight on, keeping downhill at any junctions. You pass a SMALL CHURCH on the right. Walk through a large square with a CHURCH on the left and a *cafeneion* on the right. Follow the 'DIKTAMOS GORGE' sign ahead — slightly left.

The road leads through orange groves and soon passes a small PICNIC AREA on your right. Before the road crosses a concrete bridge, follow another large sign directing you left onto a dirt track. Almost immediately (after 15m/yds) drop down right into the stream bed (1; RED PAINT ARROWS) and then out again, going through a STOCK GATE. Once through the gate, you are on a rough, rock-strewn path which

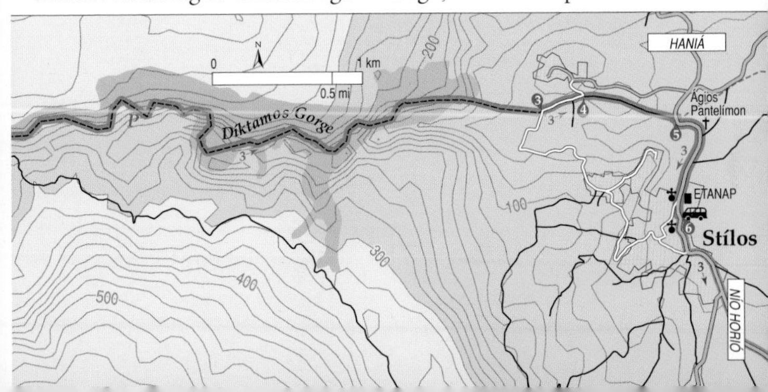

follows the stream on your left. After 30m/yds, the path becomes more distinct and is lined with stones on both edges. It soon turns left through some large shrubs and continues along the stream. It crosses a smaller watercourse leading into the main stream and passes between two wooden benches. Just past the benches, go through

another STOCK GATE (2) and enter the main part of the **Diktamos Gorge**.

The route is waymarked with what can seem rather invasive large arrows, indicating the easiest walking route. It crosses and recrosses the river bed throughout the walk. There are many places to linger and picnic. In less than **1h** the landscape opens out somewhat; then the towering sides of the gorge close in on us again. In **1h30min** the route rises up to the left and there is a makeshift handrail to help you negotiate a steep drop.

By **3h** you are out of the gorge and walking along the river bed, as the countryside opens out. The walk continues in and beside the river bed. Five minutes later the waymarking leads us up to the right, away from the oleander-lined river bed and onto a MOTORABLE TRACK (3). In three-four minutes keep straight on, where a track goes off right. A minute later the track divides; go straight on (4), on the right-hand side of the river bed. Just over 500m further on, the track goes back into the river bed for 50m, then heads up left, to a BRIDGE ON THE MAIN ROAD (5).

Turn right over the bridge, pass a SHRINE to St Pantelimon and walk on past the huge ETANAP Samaria water bottling plant, into **Stilos** (**3h35min**). There is a BUS STOP (6) opposite the large shady open area, outside a *cafeneion*. Rather than wait for the late afternoon bus, why not relax in the shade here for a while and then walk to **Nio Horio** just 25 minutes away (**4h**)? Here you can pick up one of the more frequent buses or a taxi. The BUS STOP is opposite the kiosk which you will see as you approach the village.

In the depths of the leafy Diktamos Gorge

Mullein (Verbascum thapsiforme)

Spiny acanthus (Acanthus spinosus)

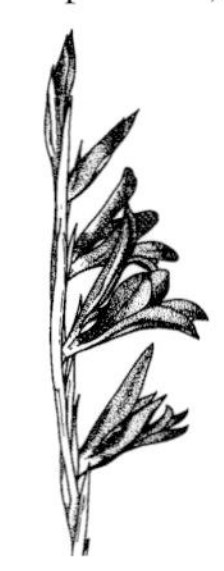

Field gladiolus (Gladiolus segetum)

Cretan ebony (Ebenus cretica)

Pomegranate (Punica granatum)

Thorny burnet (Sarcopoterium spinosum)

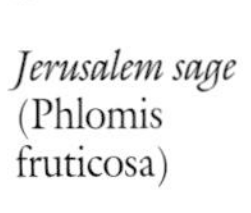

Jerusalem sage (Phlomis fruticosa)

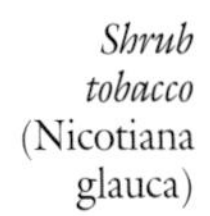

Shrub tobacco (Nicotiana glauca)

Walk 4: KAMBI • VOLIKA REFUGE • KAMBI

Distance: 14km/8.7mi; 4h55min
Grade: ● very strenuous, with a height difference of about 770m/2525ft
Equipment: walking boots, long trousers, long socks, windproof, sunhat, compass or GPS, picnic, water
Picnic: just outside Kambi
Access: 🚗 to/from Kambi; park near the church where the walk starts (35° 25.078'N, 24° 4.178'E). There is a bus (see Walk 3) but times are not convenient and there is no same day return.
Alternative return: ● You could descend on the shepherds' dirt road from near the Volika hut. It winds gently downhill, with spectacular views over the coast. Beyond **Madaro** (ⓐ), you will be on asphalt until you reach **Kambi**. This descent adds 4km/2.5mi, making the walk 18km/11mi; under 6h.

If you have come to Crete prepared to spend some nights away from your base, consider staying in Kambi the night before starting this hike. It's a very pleasant, quiet village with a relaxed atmosphere. There is a bus up to Kambi at crack of dawn, but as this trek is a real energy-tester, you might find it helpful to be on the spot in the early morning ... particularly if you fancy turning it into an expedition.* As the success of this walk relies on compass readings (unless you are using our GPS files), do choose a clear day, when the mountains are easily visible and the views are sure to be good. The route up to Volika is now waymarked with E4 signs. Some are on poles, but many are large yellow, white and black circular 'poached eggs' painted on rocks. This has made the ascent and descent much easier, but it is still a good idea to use a compass or GPS and look out for the features mentioned in the description.

The bus stops in the square in **Kambi**, by the CHURCH. **Set off** (**O**): walk right, past the church, on an asphalt road signposted to Madaro and the Volika Shelter. (The bus continues in the same direction towards Madaro.) Walk to the right of a defunct, vine-covered *cafeneion* and take a compass reading on the corner. Face the mountains towards which you are heading, which are due south, and notice, in particular, the tree-covered slopes of the ravine, which is south-southwest from this point. Then continue on the road, disregarding a track to the left passed a few minutes later. Pass a house that has rows of potted plants and flowers along its length, and a SHRINE — both on the right.

Directly afterwards, at a junction, fork right on a road, following signposting for 'PSYCHRO PIGADI, THYMIA'. (There is also a signpost in Greek: 'Τερο Πρινοζ Ψυχρο Πηγαδι Θυμια'. Some 200m further on, at the next junction (❶), go left between TWO OLIVE TREES and walk

*You could hire a guide to show you the area *beyond* the Volika hut, which is our point of return. Taking your own provisions, you would stay overnight at the hut (which is otherwise locked). You can arrange this via the EOS office at 90 Tzanakaki Street in Hania (tel: 28210 44647; www.eoshanion.gr).

slightly uphill, towards houses on the edge of the village. Go right at the houses (now on a track, signposted in Greek to 'Βολικα') and then left at the next turn, past a VINEYARD. Down to the right is a PICNIC AREA, with a map.

The track runs out in front of a concrete farm building (❷; **20min**). Take the signposted 'VOLIKA' footpath that leads steeply uphill here, guided by E4 waymarking. Initially there is fencing on the left, but very soon this stops. Fencing starts on the right, and your route runs quite near it. About five minutes from the start of the path, look out for a MAKESHIFT GATE. Notice a line of four low 'bumpy' hills on your left in the distance; the gate, set at an angle, is in line with the second 'bump', and the barbed wire that has topped the fence breaks for the gate. Turn round here and get your bearings for the return. *This is important*. Beyond Souda Bay, in the

View towards the Volika hut, on the final approach

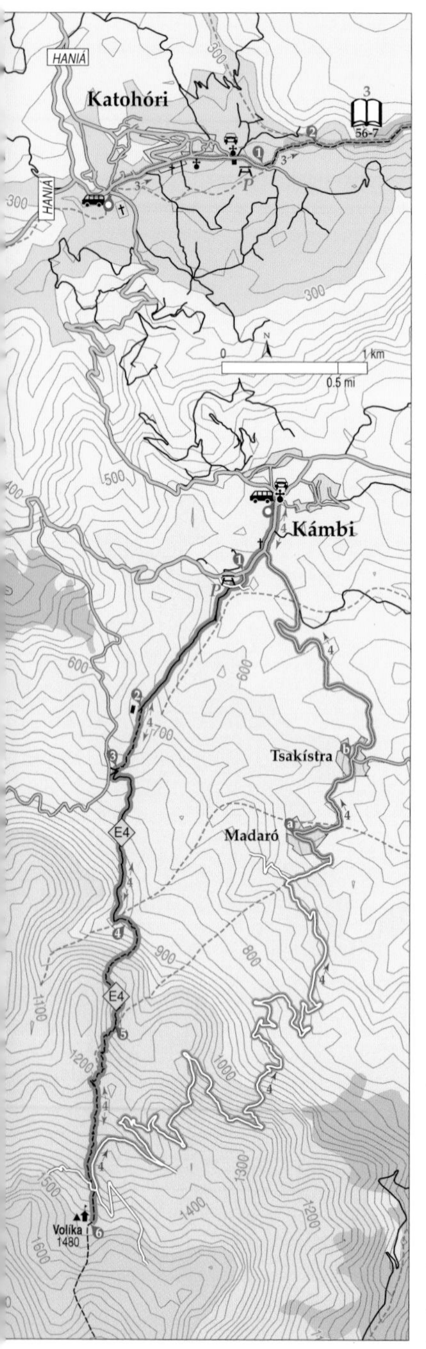

distance, the Akrotiri airport mast is visible. At the left end of the same peninsula, where the mountainside seems to fall into the sea, is Stavros (shown on page 27). Further left, pick out the island of Theodorou, just off the north coast at Platanias and, beyond that, the Rodopou Peninsula. *Then take note of Kambi's position very carefully.* These precautions are to save you wading through thistles and thorny burnet on your way back down to the village.

Setting off again, your route continues uphill. You come up onto a track (❸; where there is an asphalt road over to the right). Follow the track uphill and, 15 minutes later, as you round a bend, you will see the track bending left, cutting across a wooded ravine ahead. There is a stock control gate on the bend. From this point the mountains are spread before you, and this is a good place to get your bearings — you can see the Volika hut up on the mountainside in the ravine you are aiming for, as well as the last curve of the track above Madaro (to the left of the hut).

Some 200m/yds after the bend, take the path striking off right uphill (❹; signpost: 'BOΛIKA'). Five minutes later you will be at the TOP OF THIS RISE. Look ahead: there is one prominent, domed mountain which has trees down the left-hand side of its top. Two 'bumps' from that one, to the left, find a mountain with trees all over its summit. The route to the refuge is via the V-SHAPED RAVINE WITH TREES DOWN BOTH ITS SLOPING SIDES.

From the top of the rise continue by walking north-northwest towards the ravine and the ascent route to Volika. After the top of the rise, head south towards a circular pasture area and scramble up some

rocks to the right. Keep heading towards the ravine, going via more CIRCULAR PASTURES and keeping an eye out for the 'poached egg' waymarking.

By **1h30min**, having negotiated some sharp, pale grey rock, you look up the ravine and towards the final ascent. The good waymarking now leads you up the very steep right-hand side of the ravine. Trees provide shade and resting places. After climbing for 20 minutes or so, the path leads you to the other (left) side of the ravine (➎; **1h50min**). Ten minutes later it crosses back to the right. Some 35 minutes from starting up the ravine (**2h25min**), come to a flat wooded area: the ravine appears to end here, but follow the waymarking uphill.

The ravine becomes a gully, wedged in beside layered rock to the left of the route. Just under an hour from the start of the final ascent the Volika hut comes into sight. Five minutes later the path crosses the gully on the layered rock. E4 poles are there to guide you. Looking at your destination, approach it from the left to find easiest access. By **3h10min** you have the satisfaction of reaching the **Volika** HUT (➏). Apart from the new track — which is invasive right up here, but which has been made to aid shepherding — you feel miles from anywhere.

The return along your outward route should take much less time, although a large proportion of it requires careful walking and close attention to direction. It will take about an hour to get to the bottom of the ravine. Make your way back and, on the far side of the ravine, head due north — not northeast. Be sure to go far enough in a northerly direction before turning towards Kambi; wait until you can actually see the village and route on which you started the climb, before heading back down to **Kambi** (◯; **4h55min**).

Or descend by the alternative route; this adds 4km, but the views are wonderful.

Walk 5: GEORGIOUPOLI CIRCUIT

See also photo on page 34
Distance: 14km/8.7mi; 4h
Grade: ● straightforward climb/descent of 350m/1150ft, but with *faint and overgrown paths to locate and negotiate;* almost *no* shade
Equipment: walking trainers, sunhat, picnic, water, swimming things, ***long trousers/sleeves***
Picnic: Georgioupoli harbourside, chapel shown on page 34 or beach (no shade); Exopolis church (shade, benches)

Access: Rethimnon/Iraklion 🚌 (Timetables 1, 2) to/from Georgioupoli; journey time 45min. Or 🚗: park near Georgioupoli Square (35° 21.770'N, 24° 15.588'E).
Shorter walk: Circuit from Argirimouri (8km/5mi; 2h45min). ● Grade, equipment as main walk. Access by 🚗 car: park near Georgia Taverna in Argirimouri (35° 22.481'N, 24° 14.836'E) and pick up the walk at ❷ (the 45min-point).

Georgioupoli is a pleasant place for walking, eating, swimming and relaxing. At the end of this walk, you might like to cross the highway to the lake at Kournas (Walk 6) for a swim or quiet lakeside taverna meal.

From the GEORGIOUPOLI BUS STOP (ⓐ) on the A90 NATIONAL HIGHWAY, cross the road and take the road almost opposite into **Georgioupoli**. Follow the road straight across the VILLAGE SQUARE (○), where the **walk begins**. Keep ahead down over a BRIDGE spanning the fishing harbour. There's a lovely view out to sea on your right and up to the mountains on your left. Ignoring minor turns left and right, stay on this main road — past garishly painted 'Morfi Village' — until you reach GEORGIA TAVERNA at **Argirimouri** (**❶**; **45min**). Turn right off the road here, walk in front of the taverna, and then take a single-lane road off left, just beside the taverna.

The asphalt road becomes a concrete track and climbs steeply (**50min**), past a large house on the left. After a couple more minutes, the concrete reverts to earthen track. Just ahead and slightly left, a stock control gate may be labelled 'PATH TO LIKOTINARA'. Go through the gate and emerge in a small clearing. (This *may* be your first taste of overgrown path, especially if it's early spring.)

Ahead is a TREE WITH FADED RED WAYMARKS and ROCKS WITH BLUE WAYMARKS; your path passes between the tree and rocks and winds uphill; *watch carefully for the occasional cairn,* as well as blue or red paint waymarks on the rocks.

After a few more minutes, pass through a STOCK CONTROL GATE in a fence (blue waymark). The path becomes more distinct and the views open out. In 10 minutes, there is a broken DRYSTONE WALL on your right. When the path splits, take the right-hand path, rising up alongside the wall. *Keep watch for cairns and occasional waymarks* as the path heads north-northeast up the hillside. As you are nearing the top, the path passes an old LIME PIT on the right.

The path rises to a TRACK (❷; **1h25min**), where you go left. After a few minutes the roofs of Likotinara come into view, and the sea is seen to the right. Some 10-15 minutes later strike off right on a small concrete track which soon becomes a single-lane road, and head down towards Likotinara. In eight minutes, having wound through olive groves and past some old,

The shady terrace viewpoint at Exopolis church makes a good picnic perch.

ruined houses, you meet the road in **Likotinara** (**1h50min**). Turn right and walk to the VIEWPOINT (❸) over the coast and distant mountains. There is a monument here to Communist Resistance fighters.

Returning from the viewpoint, keep right along the village road past the turning where you came in. At the fork under 500m from the viewpoint, go left towards 'LITSARDA' and 'VAMOS' (❹; Kefalas is signposted to the right). Pass a sign indicating you are leaving Likotinara and, eight minutes later, come to the start of **Selia** (**2h05min**). Follow the main road into the village, ignoring any turns left or right.

Then, opposite a BASKETBALL COURT and by a small SHRINE at the corner of a house, turn left on a track (❺; asphalted for the first 50m/yds). Follow it to a large house, and then turn immediately left (faded blue dot waymark on the wall) on what is now a two wheeled track with an accompanying water pipe. In a couple of minutes go through a stock control gate, after which the track continues to the left. Do *not* follow it; instead, just through the gate, both you and the water pipe take the path to the right, meandering down the hillside. *Although this path is well waymarked with blue dots, it may be heavily overgrown (depending on the time of year).* In a few minutes, you will see the main asphalt road; just continue on the path, parallel with the road and slightly above it. *Or escape to the road if you're finding it too overgrown to continue.* Some **2h20min** into the walk, you will see the sea again at Georgioupoli.

The path widens, as it comes down towards a HAIRPIN BEND in the road by a broken stone wall (❻; **2h25min**). Turn left here to continue on a wide dirt track. *But this is a good place to join the road, in view of more scratchy vegetation when*

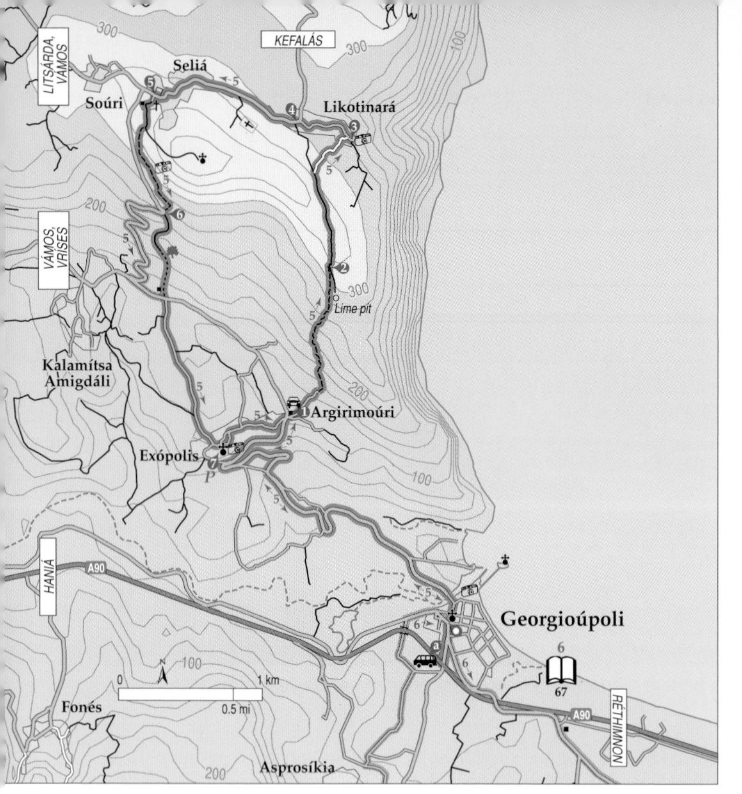

*the track ends about 10 minutes ahead.** In two minutes you will go through a stock control gate, followed quickly by another one as you head downhill. After another six or seven minutes, the dirt track ends in an OLIVE GROVE. Go straight ahead through the olive grove and find the best path you can down the hillside towards a SMALL FARM BUILDING beside the asphalt road. The path is *very* overgrown and prickly in places, but you need only persevere for about 300m/yds. If you *do* persevere with the path, you will walk past the front of the farm building, now apparently abandoned (**2h50min**). The way becomes a concrete track and meets the main road.

Cross over and take the small road signed 'EXOPOLI'. Walk up to **Exopolis** (**3h**). When the narrow road forks, keep straight ahead (left). Then, at the T-junction, turn turn right, to pass the VILLAGE CHURCH (7) on your right. This is a good place to stop for a break or a picnic, with benches in the shade and fine views both inland and seaward.

From the church continue on the narrow road through the village houses and very soon you will see Georgioupoli down to the right. Follow the narrow road down to Georgia Taverna *(where the Shorter walk ends)*. Now retrace your steps back to the bridge and then through **Georgioupoli** (O; **4h**). Allow another 10 minutes if you're walking back to the BUS STOP (a).

*If you pick up the road at this bend, when you meet the road coming from Georgioupoli, turn left (right goes to Kalamitsa and Amigdali) and walk downhill for a few minutes, then turn right on the road signed to 'EXOPOLI', 1km away. Pick up the main walk there, at the church (7).

Walk 6: LAKE KOURNAS CIRCUIT

See also photo on page 34
Distance: 12km/7.6mi; 3h30min
Grade: ● easy-moderate; an easy climb of 150m/500ft on an asphalt road, then a gentle descent of 150m/500ft on dirt tracks.
Equipment: walking trainers, sunhat, picnic, water, swimming things
Picnic: Lake Kournas
Access: Rethimnon/Iraklion 🚌 (Timetables 1, 2) to/from Georgioupoli; journey time 45min. Or 🚗: park near Georgioupoli Square (35° 21.770'N, 24° 15.588'E).

This is a pleasant — fairly easy but longish — walk through villages and countryside around the resort area of Georgioupoli. The focal point is the lake at Kournas — the only *natural* fresh-water lake on Crete (Lake Agia visited on Walk 1

Start out at the BUS STOP on the A90 NATIONAL HIGHWAY (◉) opposite the Georgioupoli turn-off. Cross the road and walk towards **Georgioupoli**. About two minutes (150m/yds) from the highway, and *before* you reach Georgioupoli village centre, turn sharp right (almost back on yourself), following signposting to 'RETHYMNO' and 'KOURNAS'. Leaving Georgioupoli (**5min**), and close to a petrol station, continue on the main road which swings right and crosses over the highway by a BRIDGE.

Once over the bridge, the road swings left and you continue along it, now parallel with the highway. At a junction (**15min**), there is a slip road left onto the highway and a taverna ahead of you. Follow your road around to the right. At **20min**

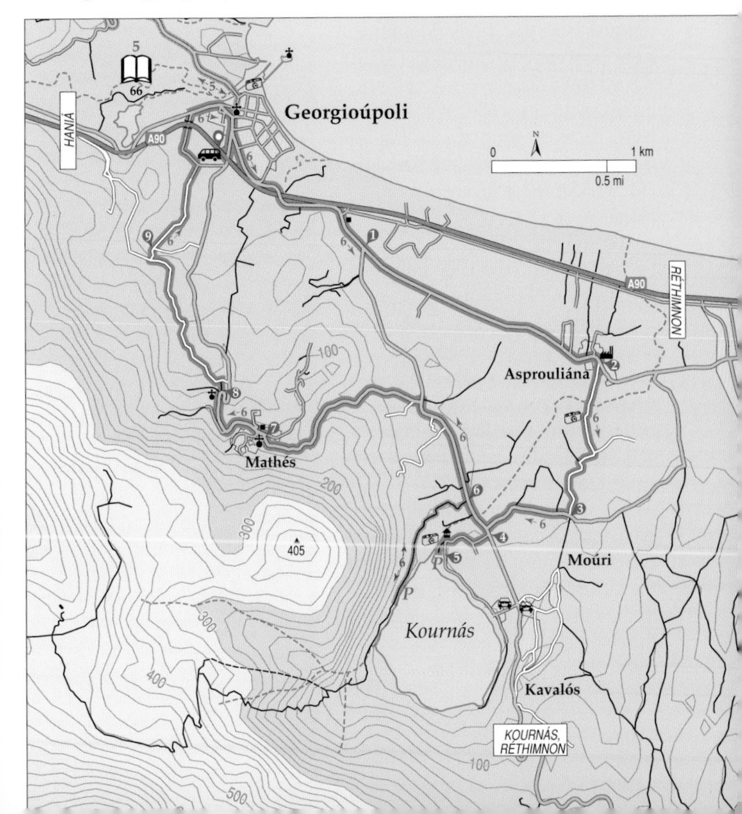

continue straight ahead towards 'KAVROS' (❶), *ignoring* a sign right to Lake Kournas. This road continues straight ahead through olive groves until it reaches the village of **Asprouliana** (**35min**). Shortly after walking past a new housing development, the old village begins. Opposite a FACTORY BUILDING on your left (❷; **45min**), take a dirt track heading obliquely right. As you walk along this track through olive groves and fields, the White Mountains rise impressively ahead of you. About 10 minutes after starting on this track (700m), ignore a track off to the left.

Eventually your track meets an asphalt road at an intersection (❸;**1h10min**). Turn right. About 10 minutes later, at a T-junction, turn left. Then turn right after just 40m/yds, following signposting for Lake Kournas (❹; **1h20min**). *Note this point for your return.* A couple of minutes later, at a T-junction, turn right between two buildings (again signed 'LAKE KOURNAS'). In a few minutes, just by a BIRDWATCHING HIDE, there is a footpath leading down to the edge of **Lake Kournas** (❺; **1h35min**), a lovely place to picnic.

From here retrace your steps back to the junction at ❹ and now turn left for 'GEORGIOUPOLI'. Ignore tracks left and right into fields. (But after 250m/yds, you might like to turn left on a TRACK (❻) and follow it as long as you like, for an even better view of the lake; the distance and time for this detour are *not* included in the main walk.)

Eventually, turn left uphill on asphalt at the sign for 'MATHES' (**1h50min**). As you ascend towards the village, the scenery begins to change from the flat coastal plain of the first half of the walk. You are soon edging a small ravine, pleasantly green and tree-covered.

Arriving in **Mathes** (**2h25min**), follow the main road through the village, passing the Mathes Taverna on your right and the main village CHURCH (❼) opposite the taverna on your left. Five minutes after leaving the village, and just after another CHURCH, the asphalt road makes a sharp hairpin bend to the right. Just before the apex of this bend, take the worn, NARROW DIRT TRACK (❽) heading *downhill* on your left. (*Do not* take the dirt track leading left *up*hill just after the church and before this track.) Two minutes later, at a T-junction with a good dirt road, turn left.

This track meanders pleasantly through more olive groves before turning sharp right (where there is a house ahead; **3h05min**). About 100m/yds further on, the track forks. Take the left fork (❾). As you arrive at the outskirts of Georgioupoli, the

dirt track becomes a single-lane asphalt road. At a T-junction turn left (**3h15min**). The road soon bends round to the right and goes through a tunnel under the highway and into **Georgioupoli**. At the next T-junction, turn right on the main road into the village. At the HOTEL DROSIA (**3h25min**) take the right fork towards the village centre. A short way along, at the T-junction with the main road through the village, turn right. At the next junction, take the right fork, back to the BUS STOP on the NATIONAL HIGHWAY (**O**), where the walk began (**3h30min**).

Lake Kournas is a very popular recreational area with the locals and tourists alike. You can swim, rent pedaloes and other water sports equipment, laze about at a taverna … or feed the geese.

Walk 7: THE PRASSANOS GORGE

Distance: 10.6km/6.6mi; 3h30min *(allow a good 5h; see under 'Grade')*
Grade: ● moderate, but you must be sure-footed and agile. Basically an overall descent of somewhat over 250m/820ft. ***Important:*** Outside high summer, if there has been a bad winter, or heavy rainfall (enquire locally), ***the gorge is not passable.*** The walk is best kept for June to September.
Equipment: walking trainers, sunhat, picnic, water
Picnic: anywhere in the gorge
Access: Rethimnon or Iraklion 🚌 (Timetables 1, 2) to the Rethimnon bus station; journey time 1h. Then take either a 🚗 taxi or an Amari 🚌 (not in the timetables, but departs 14.00 Mon/Wed/Fri *only*); journey time 30min. Ask for 'Prassanos' (the gorge) or Mirthios. Return on town 🚌 from Missiria (every 15min); journey time 30min
Short walk: Prassanos Gorge from Missiria (distance and time immaterial). Equipment and picnic as main walk. Access by 🚗: drive from Rethimnon to Missiria and, just before the bridge over the Prassanos outlet, turn right for Gianoudi (signed in Greek, Γιανουδι). Go under the national highway, and turn left at the T-junction. The road curves right. At a Y-fork go left and keep following the stream (eventually on a stabilised track), until you come to a parking place at the right of the CONCRETE BRIDGE (4; 35° 20.456'N, 24° 32.450'E). Walk *up* the gorge as far as you like and return the same way.

This gorge is an awe-inspiring and inviting sight as it carves a swathe through the countryside to the coast by Rethimnon. It has obviously been created by great force — as you'll see from the massive boulders en route. The landscape around is very open and pleasing to look at, making a good, accessible walk. But save it for the summer months — you don't want to get halfway down the gorge and find yourself having to swim or walk all the way back up! If you go out of 'season', then the Short walk may be the answer.

The taxi or bus will drop you at a road junction where a sign indicates 'MIRTHIOS' off to the right. From this junction (O), **start out** by walking 300m/yds towards AMARI along the road. Then turn left on a CONCRETE TRACK (1). Immediately you are facing the huge entrance to the gorge; the landscape is tremendous here, open and grand. Just before the concrete runs out, in under 100m, open the wire gate and go through. You may see a sign on this gate or the next one indicating 'no entry': you can safely ignore this, ***but please close and re-secure any gates!*** (The farmer who owns the buildings a short way ahead once told us he put up the sign out of frustration with walkers who left gates open; he does not mind walkers who behave according to the country code.)

Continue down the track. Pass through a STOCK CONTROL GATE and walk to the left of the FARM BUILDINGS (**12min**), going straight over the 'yard' and passing through a SECOND STOCK CONTROL GATE. ***Please ensure both gates are firmly re-secured.***

Now keep on downhill, on a track which runs under electricity

View to the Prassanos Gorge from near the start of the walk

wires and loops down towards a watercourse. When the track forks (**15min**), head left.

In a minute you come to the stream bed: cross it, and then cross over another, larger, stream bed lined with plane trees. Follow the narrow track round to the right, to a FENCE. Then take the path along the left-hand side of the fence. Soon (**19min**) cross a stream bed which runs down from the ridge on your left. Keep following the path beside the fence, to pass a first E4 MARKER POLE (❷) and then a SECOND E4 MARKER POLE (**22min**). Your track, still following the fence, widens slightly at this point. One minute later (**23min**) a fenced area is directly in front of you, with a sign, 'Please close the door'. But *do not* go through this gate. Instead, follow the path heading right along the side of this new fence, passing an E4 MARKER POLE WITH TWO ARROWS. After about 20m/yds, the fence turns sharply left. At this point scramble *carefully* down the steep bank to the watercourse below, taking any one of the faint sheep trails. Then follow the watercourse to the left, towards the mouth of the gorge. Very soon you will reach the main river bed which has water in it for most of the year. Cross the river at this point and head for the LARGE CONCRETE CYLINDER with an E4 ARROW (❸; **25min**) ahead and slightly to the left, in the middle of the river bed. This is the start of the **Prassanos Gorge**. *There are no more E4 signs en route.*

Some **33min** into the walk, a wall of the gorge rears up dramatically on your left. At **40min** the river bed swings left (northwest), and proceeds amongst smooth white boulders. Fantastic rock faces are now all round. When you are confronted with a huge rock face ahead, the river bed swings 90° to the left, and you encounter some really big boulders, two of which form a kind of opening through which you pass. There may well be birds of prey hovering overhead here.

Before long (**48min**) the gorge looks impassable: a 2.5m/8ft drop is in front of you. To avoid it, retrace your steps until you find an easy scramble up the right-hand side of the gorge. Scramble up about 20m/yds and look for a goat trail

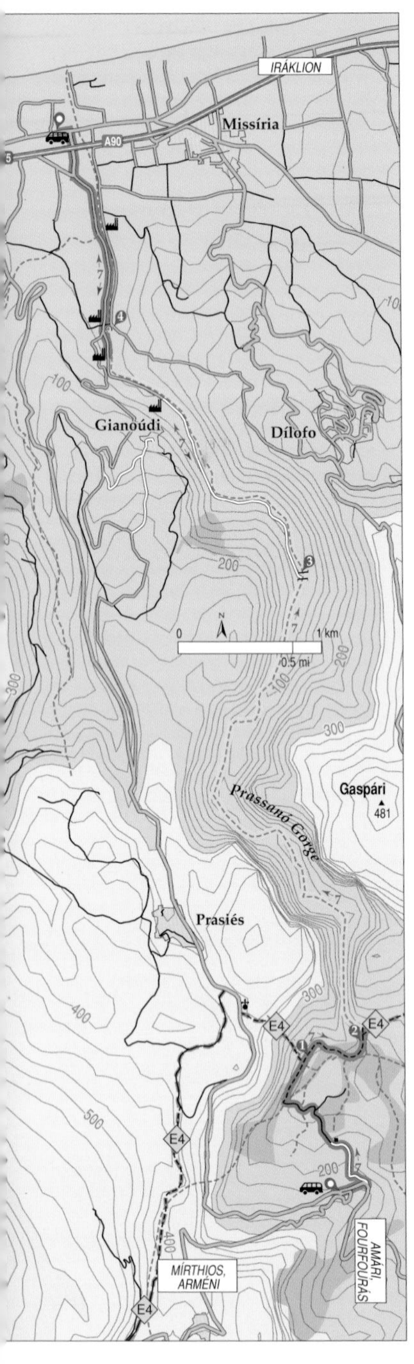

marked by cairns. Follow the trail for 100m/yds or so, until it eventually meets the river bed further on. This detour takes about 15 minutes. Now just enjoy the splendour of the gorge; unless there has been recent storm damage, there aren't any more sections as awkward as the one just avoided — although there are a few more climbs/drops from boulder to boulder before the way eases out.

The gorge narrows (**1h20min**), and the river bed is gravelly underfoot. You reach the LAST NARROW PASS (**1h50min**) where the gorge is no more than 4m/12ft wide. Fifteen minutes later (**2h05min**) you will be beyond the main part of the gorge, but still on the river bed. You come to a CONCRETE ROAD BRIDGE across the gorge (❹; **2h20min**): walk under the bridge through one of the six circular 'arches' and continue down the gorge. *(From this point on, there is a dirt road on your left. If you are tired, or want a change from walking on boulders, scramble up the bank to this road. It eventually becomes the asphalt road to Missiria.)*

Later you pass some olive groves on the left (**2h30min**). The groves and some greenhouses are dotted between a few factories from here to the mouth of the gorge. At the first factory (at time of writing) the dirt road becomes asphalted.

Continue down the river bed until it bends to the right (**3h**). Just after this bend, watch for a faint dirt and concrete track leading left, out of the river bed (above you, on the bank, there is an auto parts supplier). Take this track, then turn right on the road, passing a very attractive gently arching BRIDGE (❺) spanning the river bed (almost hidden in greenery). Continue past more factories and a manege.

Some 250m beyond the manege,

Above: near the end of the walk — or the start of the Short walk. Below: the bridge not far above the manege is hidden in greenery (left); in the depths of the gorge (right)

fork right, to walk under the A90 NATIONAL HIGHWAY and then meet the old main road to Rethimnon in the village of **Missiria**. Turn left on the road: 150m/yds along, on the right-hand side of the road, there is a BUS STOP (⑥; **3h30min**) by a parade of shops — the small sign is on an electricity pole. Alternatively, you can hail a taxi on this road.

Walk 8: VRISSINAS, MINOAN PEAK SANCTUARY

See also photo on page 79
Distance: 10km/6.3mi; 3h45min
Grade: ● moderate, with an ascent/descent of 600m/1970ft; some blue, some red and some E4 waymarks …
Equipment: walking trainers, sunhat, picnic, water, long trousers
Picnic: at the summit or the Kapadiana spring
Access: 🚌 from Rethimnon to Chromonastiri (not in the timetables; departs 06.50 Mon-Fri *only;* returns 14.40). Or 🚗: park just uphill from the bus stop at the fork where the walk goes right to the square and ahead is signed to the Military Museum (35° 19.626'N, 24° 30.715'W)

Short walk: Vrissinas summit (● under 1km; ascent/descent only 60m/200ft; allow 30min). Access by 🚗: park just below the summit and take the tightly zigzagging path to the top. Drive from Rethimnon via Agia Irini and Roussospiti towards Kapadiana. Take the second right turn after Roussospiti, with a green and yellow sign in Greek for the summit chapel of Ag Pnevma (I.N. ΑΓ. ΠΝΕΥΜΑΤΟΣ). Time, distance and ascent shown are from the car park just below the summit (accessible in 4WD), but you will have to stop sooner if you are in a normal hire car — perhaps on or near the road to the transmitters.

This is one of those hikes that give a great sense of achievement and a fantastic view. And it's particularly satisfying to see the mountain from all around and know that you've been up there! The local people make pilgrimages to Vrissinas at Easter and other festivals.

The hike begins at the BUS STOP (⓪) just above the FOOTBALL GROUND in **Chromonastiri**. Follow the road south uphill for 70m/yds, and take the first right turn. Then turn left almost at once, heading up to 'PRINARIS MILL' (a delightful museum to visit on your return). Turn right, with the mill on your left, and walk ahead for 50m, then turn right into an alley — then left and right again within a few metres. At a T-junction, turn left for a few paces, then go left again, uphill. At the next T-junction, go sharp right downhill on a concrete lane.

After 100m you cross straight over a road (where a left leads to the Military Museum). Now a cobbled path takes you down into a verdant, plane-shaded valley, past an orange grove. You cross two small CONCRETE BRIDGES (❶; **10min**) and rise up on a concrete track. At the next T-junction, turn *very* sharp left — heading back in the direction you've just come. Then, at a Y-fork, go right.

With a hillside to your right and a ravine down to the left, follow this track for 650m — to a pretty WHITE-WASHED CHURCH (❷) on your right, with benches in its courtyard. (Walk 9 passes here, following the track in the opposite direction.) Go left at the fork in front of the church, then immediately right. You join the road to **Kapadiana**, but ignore the branch on the right into the village. About 100m further on, the road crosses a stream. Set off to the left here is the leafy, cool open PICNIC AREA (❸; **30min**) shown overleaf. About 30m along the stream there's a SPRING.

Behind the spring red waymarking leads you off to the left. Within two to three minutes

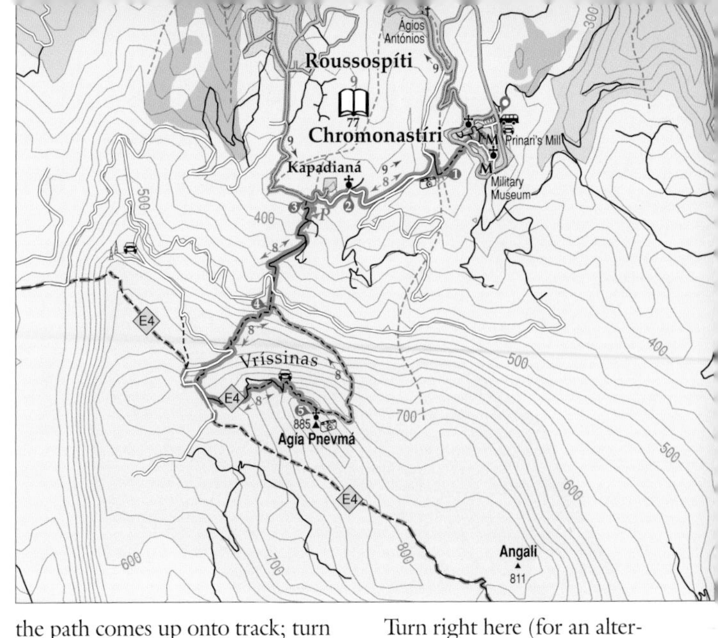

the path comes up onto track; turn right and walk up the track. Go right at the next junction. Some 200m further on, at a Y-fork, go right. In a good 10 minutes (550m) you cross straight over another wide track, to take a red-waymarked path. This rises to a fork in a few minutes (❹; **1h**).

Turn right here (for an alternative return, you could come back from the path to the left; see text below). Walk up the steep north side of the mountain. Some 15 minutes up, you go through fencing via a gate. Then the path rises to another track, where you turn left, round a hairpin bend.

Vrissinas from Kapadiana

Spring just west of Kapadiana

After 300m on this track, go half-left on a short-cut path which rejoins the track higher up.

Now go left for about 150m (some 50m past an E4 pole), then fork left on a lesser track. From here on black and yellow E4, as well as blue dot waymarks will guide you to the summit. Just before a bend to the left take another short-cut path. Then, from a level area (where you may see some vehicles parked), the path rises the final way in tight zigzags (where you may see the odd red waymark as well!) to a CHAPEL, **Agio Pnevma**, on the highest peak of the **Vrissinas** SUMMIT (➎; **2h**). There are wonderful views over the north coast and Rethimnon, with Kapadiana and Chromonastiri far below. On clear days in spring the snow-capped White Mountains and Psiloritis are on view.

Most hikers return the same way, but you could try this alternative to make a small circuit; times are about the same (2h). Leave the fenced-off chapel by the same gate through which you entered, and walk right (southeast) alongside the fencing. Guided by red waymarks, make your way diagonally downhill across the slope. In 10 minutes you reach an earthen track, which you follow to the left (red waymarks). After about 150m the track peters out into a clear path gently descending the north slope of Vrissinas. Straight ahead is a high transmitter mast, and to the right, below you, are wonderful views of Roussospiti, as well as the familiar Kapadiana and Chromonastiri.

Back at your upward route by the fork in the path (➍; **3h**), take the shady path downhill. Remember to go straight on at the first track, left at the second, and left again at the T-junction. Some 50m after going under telephone wires you leave the wide track and head left on a narrow path, back to the to the PICNIC AREA (➌; **1h15min**). If you can't remember the way back from here, see Walk 9 overleaf to return to **Chromonastiri** (⭘; **3h45min**).

Walk 9: RETHIMNON • CHROMONASTIRI • MYLI

See also photos on pages 43, 76 and 81
Distance: 11km/6.8mi; 3h30min
Grade: ● moderate, with an ascent of under 350m/1150ft
Equipment: walking trainers, sunhat, long socks, picnic, water
Picnic: the pine wood near the walk start or the Kapadiana spring
Access: to Rethimnon bus station and back (Timetables 1, 2); journey time 1h; then taxi or town bus to the kiosk at the corner of Theotokopoulou Street on the east side of town, where the walk starts. If it is very hot it's worth avoiding the pull out of town by taking a bus or taxi to the Agia Irini Monastery. Return by from Myli (not in the timetables; departs 14.55, 16.55, 18.55, 20.55 daily), or taxi from Myli (telephone for one on arrival), or tack on Walk 9.

This walk takes in a busy seaside town and two old villages — one of them still without a through road, the other with two museums well worth your visit. And you have the option to extend it through a wonderful gorge, by following Walk 10 back down to the coast.

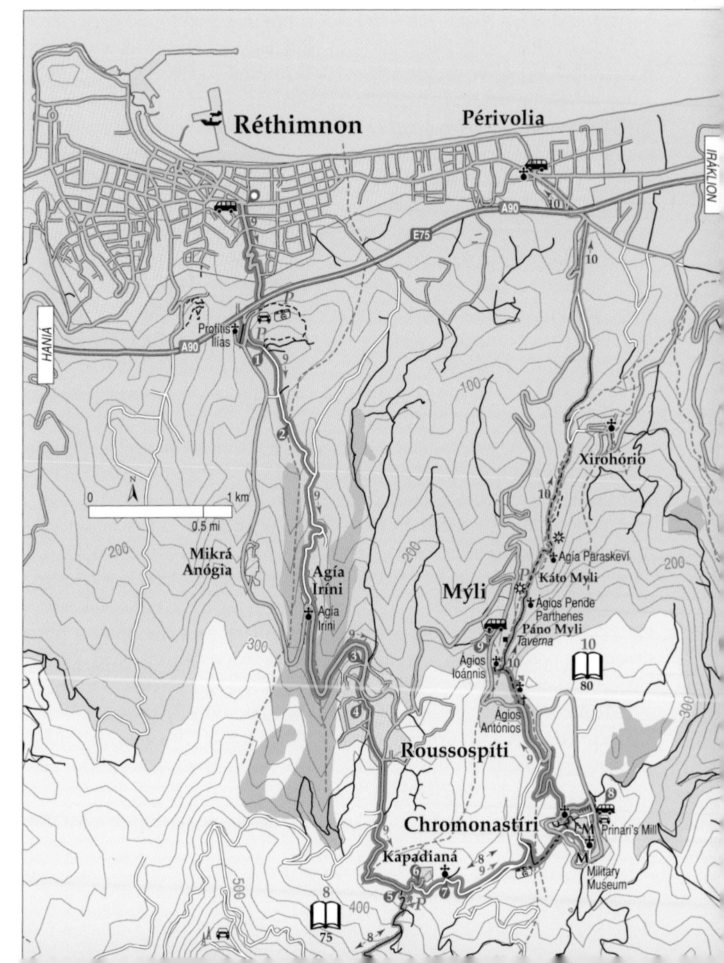

Start out east of **Rethimnon** centre, at a road junction with a blue road sign on the right to 'ROUSOSPITI' and a brown sign to 'AG EIRINI NUNNERY'). There is a kiosk on the corner, after which you will see the street name — THEOTOKOPOULOU STREET (O). Walk straight on up the hill, past a SCHOOL on the left, ignoring turnings left and right and going under the national highway. You'll soon see the small church of **Profitis Ilias** perched on a hill. At the first hairpin bend after passing under the highway (**15min**), there are fine views back over Rethimnon from a lovely picnic setting in fresh-smelling pine woods off to the left.

Unfortunately, Profitis Ilias has been fenced off in recent years and is now inaccessible, so ignore it and instead fork left *before* the church — going steeply uphill on an asphalted single-lane road. There is another pine wood here on your left — another pretty picnic opportunity. Ignore any trails through the pines; keep right. As the asphalt road ends, you encounter three tracks to the left (1): ignore them all; keep on this right-hand track. Soon the way levels out. Every pace immerses you further in the countyside.

Soon, ignore a turning left and keep walking through olive groves and vineyards. A minute later, where a well-concreted track leads up right and a rough track goes left just ahead of you, keep straight ahead on the main track. Shortly after this 'crossroads', your track goes steeply downhill, where it crosses a WATERCOURSE (2) and goes up the other side, soon passing some fig trees.

Meet a T-junction (**50min**) with a concreted track and turn right. The nunnery is high up in front of you, but not yet in sight. In 10 minutes (**1h**), where the main concrete track bends right, ignore a concrete track off left to a house. Walk into and through **Agia Irini** (**1h10min**). On the far side of the village, turn left downhill on an asphalt road, passing to the left of the **Agia Irini Convent**. You will become aware of a church perched far up on the top of Vrissinas, the mountain in the distance. The summit of Vrissinas, a Minoan peak sanctuary, is the goal of Walk 8.

Some **1h20min** en route, take the asphalt road which forks right and is signposted in Greek 'Καπαδιανα (Kapadiana) 2km' (3). The fork is just before the main part of **Roussospiti**, which you keep to your left. Follow the road and continue on up to the right steeply, levelling out slightly at a junction. Go straight across, veering right; then, at the cross-roads (where there are mail boxes on left), go left on an asphalted road signposted in Greek to ΑΓΙΟΥ ΦΑΝΟΥΡΙΟΥ (4).

Now, as you gently descend towards Kapadiana, you come to a small BRIDGE at the lowest point on the road (5; **1h55min**). Set off to the right here is a leafy, cool PICNIC AREA with a SPRING. Have a rest in the shade if you like, before continuing. Very shortly past the next bends (left and then right) take the track off to the right, signposted in Greek 'ΠΡΟΣ ΕΚΛΗΣΕΙΑ' (to the church; 6)'. Ignore all turnings off this track and in a few minutes you will walk past a white-washed CHURCH on the left. Just beyond the church, the track forks. Take the right-hand fork (7) and continue down this track as it skirts a hillside to the left and a wooded ravine to the right. Shortly, the track descends to a junction with another track. Continue ahead (left) on this new track.

The route opens out (**2h20min**)

and you can see Chromonastiri straight ahead. Follow the track round a bend; then, after about three minutes, take the first right turn — a tight hairpin — along an earthen track. Cross two small concrete BRIDGES. Beyond an orange grove on your left, the track becomes a mostly-cobbled path again and starts climbing towards the village.

Cross over a road (**2h45min**) — or first follow it right, to the small but impressive MILITARY MUSEUM — and walk past houses on a concreted track. Ignore all turnings left for 200m, until you come to the church of Ag Georgios on your left. Walk in front of the church and down to the shady SQUARE in **Chromonastiri**, where you'll find a taverna and the fascinating olive and rural household museum called PRINARI'S MILL.

From the square, head over to the right, to the main road. Walk past the BUS STOP (❽) on your right (a bus leaves here bound for Rethimnon at 14.40 Mon-Fri, if this suits your schedule) and turn left just past the FOOTBALL PITCH. After 200m, just after a SHRINE on the right, take the road off to the right **3h**). In spring masses of daisies line the route. When you meet the main road again, go left downhill, then follow a wide bend to the right, round the end of a deep verdant ravine filled with chestnut and fig trees.

Ten minutes after joining the road, by a parking bay and shrine (**3h20min**), take steps down to the right, into the **Myli Gorge**. You quickly come to the tiny shaded church of **Agios Antonios**. There's a spring just beyond the church, should you want to fill your bottle. Continue down, then follow the path beside, in and over the WATER CHANNEL. When it forks, go left over a concrete bridge *(or, if you are continuing on Walk 9, keep straight ahead here, down the Myli Gorge)*. For the main walk, go up the left-hand side of the ravine to explore the enchanting **Agios Ioannis** chapel, built into the rock. Then continue along the WATER CHANNEL to the main road and **Myli** BUS STOP (❾; **3h30min**). If you like, cross over the road and head up into the modern-day village.

Below, top: the olive press in Prinari's Mill; there is much else to see in this fine local museum, including memorabilia from rural households — like the pristine bedroom shown at the bottom.

Walk 10: MYLI GORGE

See also photo on page 00
Distance: 4.4km/2.7mi; 1h20min
Grade: ● gorge walk descending 250m/820ft; you must be agile for the stepping stones crossings
Equipment: walking trainers, sunhat, picnic, water
Picnic: in the gorge

Access: taxi or Chromonastiri to Myli (not in the timetables; departs Rethimnon 08.15, 10.15, 12.15, 14.15, 16.15, 18.15). The Myli bus stop is at the steps leading down into the gorge. Return by town on the coastal road at Perivolia.

Myli, the name of this wonderfully-cool, shady gorge and the virtually-deserted village beside the stream, derives from the many watermills in the area, which were active in Venetian times.

Start the walk below the modern village of **Myli,** at the BUS STOP (○) by steps leading down to the gorge. Pass the chapel of **Agios Ioannis**, built into the rock on the right, cross a concrete bridge, and come into **Pano** (upper) **Myli**, where there is a pleasant taverna (❶) with rooms). Here you can pick up an information leaflet about the gorge, its history, flora and fauna. Leave the taverna and take the slightly higher of two paths; it is cobbled and waymarked and heads north towards the sea.

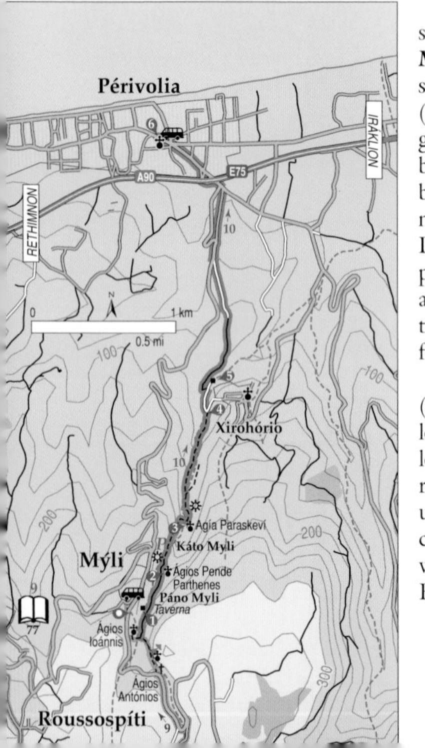

Within a couple of minutes you pass the (locked) church of **Agios Pende Parthenes** (❷) up on the right. Just after that the route becomes earthen path as it descends to the bottom of the **Myli Gorge** (**15min**), where there are many small waterfalls and ruined mills in the hillsides, once fed by the stone aqueducts that drop from mill to mill.

The path crosses to the other side of the stream at **Kato** (lower) **Myli**, and you look down on the small church of **Agia Paraskevi** (❸), on the right. After the path goes under the arch of a ruined building, you can reach the church by crossing the river bed (which might be a rushing torrent!). During the walk there are several places to cross on stepping stones, and several chapels to visit. Be sure to leave any stock control gates you find them.

The path joins a concreted track (❹; **1h**), signalling that you have left the main part of the gorge. Fork left here; pretty Xirohorio is to the right, but has no public transport, unfortunately. Before the track crosses the river bed again, you may wish to walk ahead to the 'Banana Bar' (❺) — a good place for a break (or to turn back to Myli, if you came by car). Ten minutes after crossing the river bed, you join the Myli/ Chromonastiri road: turn right and continue for just under 150m. When you come to a wide bend to the left, where there is a triangle of flowers and a telegraph pole, walk straight ahead, taking a concreted short-cut to the main road, visible below. You pass a few industrial buildings.

Five minutes downhill will bring you to a crossroads with a main road: turn left and walk downhill. The A90 national highway is over to the right; your route (which you can't see from here) takes you under the highway on a bit of pavement. Then keep left at the Y-fork (a petrol station is to the right) and walk on to a T-junction, where RETHIMNON is signposted to the left. You can catch a town bus here in **Perivolia** (**1h20min**): go left to a BUS STOP 250m along (❻), opposite a church.

Right: the church of Agia Paraskevi, and, below, the gorge not far north of the church. These photos were taken in April, when the river could have been much higher. Be prepared to cross stepping stones where bridges are felled by storms. If you wear waterproof boots — or you don't mind getting your feet wet — just wade!

Walk 11: GOUVERNETO AND KATHOLIKOU

See also photo on page 4
Distance: 4.3km/2.7mi; 1h30min
Grade: ● moderate-strenuous, with a steep descent/reascent of 260m/ 850ft; *caution and agility* required beyond Moni Katholikou
Equipment: walking trainers, sunhat, picnic, water, (swimming things — optional), ***torch***, suitable dress to enter the monastery (see page 27 for opening times).
Picnic: anywhere on the walk
Access: 🚗 to Moni Gouverneto (Car tour 4, page 26; 35° 35.075'N, 24° 8.406'E)

The Akrotiri Peninsula, mushrooming out into the sea east of Hania, invites exploration. This walk follows an ancient path, originally traced by a hermit who, in the eleventh century, founded what is considered to be the island's earliest monastery, Moni Katholikou. The descent passes some interesting sites.

Start out from the CAR PARK at **Moni Gouverneto** (**◎**): walk through the gate (open 09.00-21.00) into the monastery gardens — full of birdsong — and leave by the gate at the far end. Then take the stepped, beautifully cobbled path (by a WAR MEMORIAL) leading down the hillside towards the sea. A red arrow on a SHRINE to your left will direct you initially. In **5min** you enjoy some lovely views, especially down over the rocky coast — just one of many good places to picnic.

Further downhill, leave the path and turn right to a cool CAVE (**❶**; **10min**), with a chapel dedicated to **Panagia Arkoudiotissa** at its

entrance and a huge, bear-shaped stalagmite in its centre. It is believed that this holy place pre-dates Minoan times.

Continue down, following the clear path which starts to zigzag (**15min**). Just before you reach ruined Moni Katholikou (abandoned on account of repeated pirate raids), you can visit the large CAVE of **Agios Ioannis**

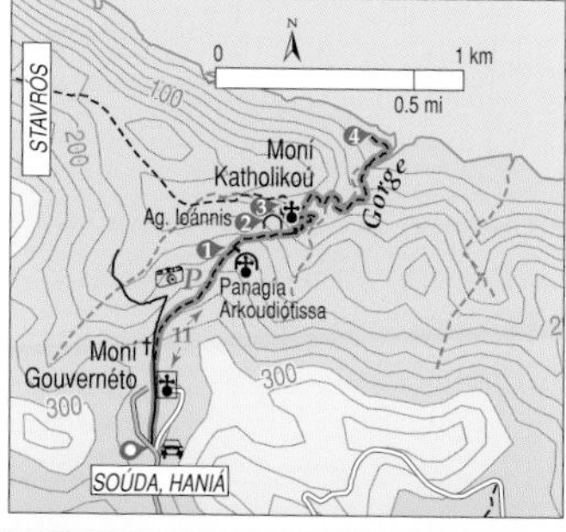

(❷) on the left; this one contains the grave of the hermit saint in its deepest recess, which you can see by torchlight.

Then descend to **Moni Katholikou** (❸; **25min**), built into the escarpment beside an impressive arched bridge over the narrow gorge. A path heads west from here to Stavros.

Should you decide to scramble down to the river bed, the path goes under the arch of the bridge (waymarked with red/white stripes). It requires caution and agility. Once down, it's 12 minutes to the rocky edge of the sea (**40min**). It's difficult to swim here unless you make your way round to the left, where there is an old quarry slipway (❹).

To return, retrace your steps to **Moni Gouverneto** (**○**; **1h30min**).

Moni Katholikou and the bridge over the gorge (left), and the inviting — but inaccessible — sea at the 40min-point. To swim, make your way to the old quarry.

Walk 12: RODOPOS • AGIOS IOANNIS GIONIS • RODOPOS

Distance: 18.5km/11.5mi; 5h30min (20.3km/12.6mi if decending to Agios Pavlos)
Grade: ● straightforward but taxing, with ups and downs totalling 550m/1800ft (670m/2200 if visiting Agios Pavlos). The initial descent is steep, and the final climb, while gradual, is long. *Very little shade en route.*
Equipment: walking trainers, sunhat, cover-up protection from the sun, picnic, plenty of water
Picnic: Agios Ioannis Gionis

Access: 🚗 to/from Rodopos; park near the square (35° 33.702'N, 23° 45.311'E). Or 🚌 to Rodopos (not in the timetables, but departs Hania 13.00, 13.20 Mon-Fri); journey time 50min. Or 🚌 to Kolimbari (Timetables 7, 8); journey time 30min, then 🚗 taxi from there to Rodopos (the taxi rank is at the main crossroads). Return with 🚗 taxi from Rodopos to Kolimbari (telephone from the *cafeneion* in the village square), then 🚌 to Hania (Timetables 7, 8).

One can't fail to notice the Rodopou Peninsula on the map of Crete, jutting out into the sea with the Gramvousa Peninsula — rather like a rabbit's ears. The peninsulas invite exploration. This walk starts and finishes in the very pleasant square in Rodopos village; all the locals collect here to pass the time of day and watch the world go by. You will be enveloped in quietness and a miles-away-from-it-all feeling on this

Landscape of the Rodopou Peninsula. This photo was taken just north of Agios Ioannis Gionis, in the Natura 2000 protection area.

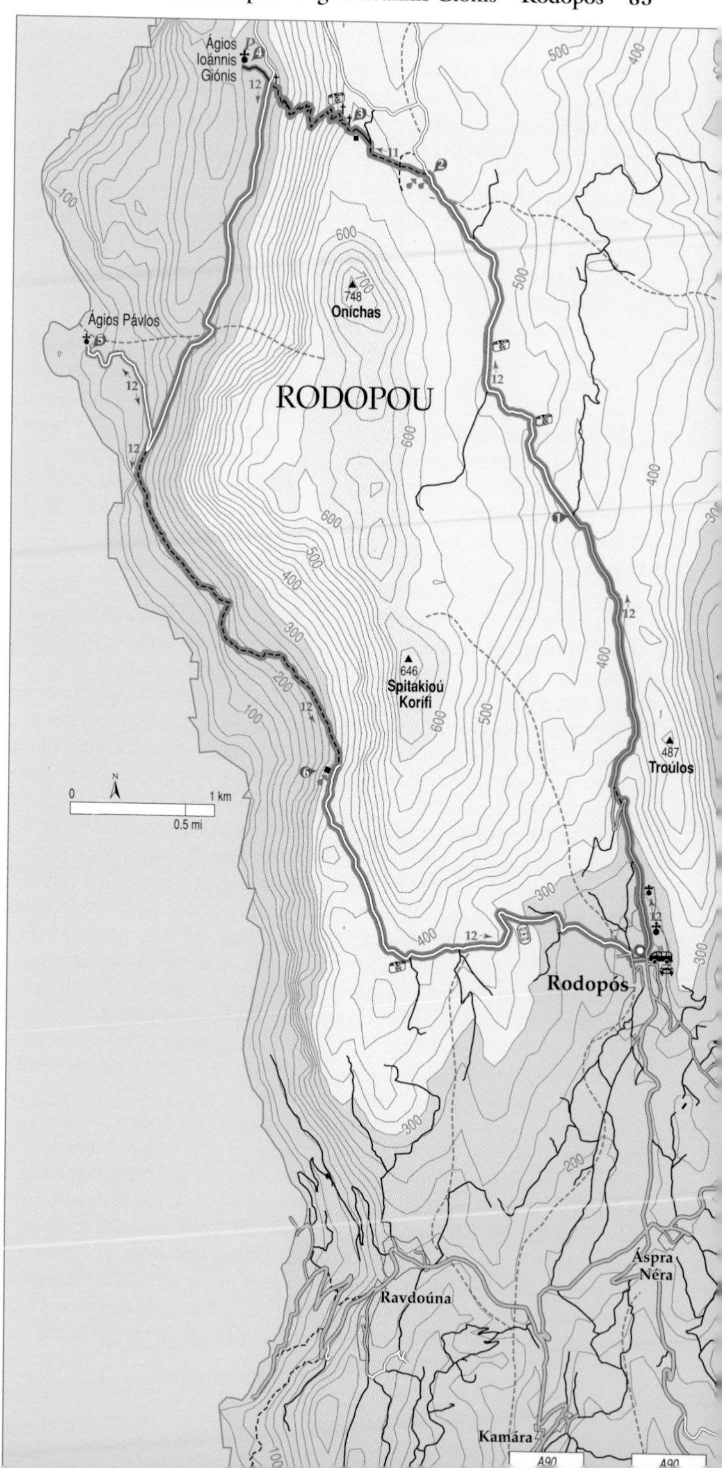
Ágios
Ioánnis
Giónis
RODOPOU
Oníchas
748
Ágios Pávlos
Spitakioú
Korífi
646
Troúlos
487
Rodopós
Ravdoúna
Áspra
Néra
Kamára
0
1 km
0.5 mi
A90

peninsula. The walk is well waymarked, and few trees obscure the route. The few trees, however, offer very little shade, so this is *not* a hike for high summer. Getting into the church of Agios Ioannis Gionis is not an essential part of the walk but, if you wish to do so, ask for the key in Rodopos.

The bus turns round at the village square at **Rodopos** (○). To **start the walk**, leave the square on your right and take the road which leads out north past a BUST (also on the right), in a corner of the square. The road takes you past a large CHURCH on the right — a good landmark when you return to the village from a different direction, at the end of the walk. Two to three minutes later, near the edge of Rodopos, pass another much smaller and very pretty CHURCH tucked back on the right. Keep straight on.

Five minutes' walking will take you out of the village. Ten minutes later (**15min**), the road starts to bend. After the first big hairpin bend to the left, look for a path going uphill to the right, with a stone wall on its left-hand side: it cuts some loops off the road. When you meet the road again, head right. Eventually tarmac gives way to gravel, as you continue in the same northerly direction. At **45min** the gravel road passes a CONCRETE PILLAR (❶). Ignore the track heading off right beyond it; go straight ahead. Ten minutes later the sea is in sight behind you and to your right. Then these views are lost, as the route bends left and inland.

After **1h** walking a track peels off left; continue on the gravel road you have been following and in another five minutes the sea will come into sight again over to the right. Soon TWO CISTERNS (❷; **1h15min**) are ahead to the left and there is a sign in Greek indicating that the way to Agios Ioannis Gionis is to the right. The sign is for *vehicles*. Head off *left* beside the cisterns, on a smaller track (more like a goats' trail — or like a stream bed after wet weather). One or two minutes (200m) past the cisterns, cross a track and continue straight on. A couple of minutes later curve round to the right. Continue round to the right and then, at a Y-fork a minute later, keep left uphill.

The track soon runs out (**1h25min**), in an open area where there is a building set down to the left. Walk straight ahead in the direction you have been heading. Then go right and find a waymark indicating a path leading to a low wall on which a METAL SHRINE (❸) is bolted. Look over the wall and you will see the gravel road you were originally following continuing downhill — to the dilapidated but attractively-sited church of Agios Ioannis Gionis far below. Secluded by trees and surrounded by open grazing land, the church is protected from the sea beyond by a ridge. To the left, the end of the Gramvousa Peninsula (photograph page 17) is visible, reaching out into the sea. Take the footpath to the left of the low wall and wind slowly downhill. Within a couple of turns you pass a MINIATURE CHURCH perched on a rock.

Some 35 minutes of careful walking on the loose earth-and-rubble path will bring you to the flat area around **Agios Ioannis Gionis** (❹; **2h15min**). To visit the church, cross the open ground in front of it. There are two concrete WCs to the left of it. The church is an obvious place to rest and picnic, in the

Some 25 minutes from Agios Ioannis Gionis, you look down to the sea and another church, Agios Pavlos. (This photograph was taken before the new gravel road to the chapel was built.)

welcome shade of a plane tree. Anyone and everyone who is called Ioannis can come here on one particular day in the year to be baptised ... that's a lot of Johns!

From here go back to the SHRINE where the footpath ended and follow the road south, past some olive groves and vineyards. Eventually Kastelli and the Kissamos Gulf come into view. Some 25 minutes from the church (**2h40min**) you look down to another church by the sea, **Agios Pavlos** (➎). Where the gravel road makes a hairpin down to the church, keep straight ahead. (Or allow an extra couple of kilometres and 120m/400ft of descent and reascent if you go down to see the church.)

Continue on across the hillside, parallel with the sea, on a cairned and occasionally waymarked path. Some 1h20min from Agios Ioannis Gionis (**3h35min**) a few trees near a ravine provide rare and welcome shade. Below, the vivid blue sea curls tantalisingly up onto the rocky coastline. A patch of small carob trees, again by a ravine, offers a further brief shady interlude. Ten to 15 minutes beyond here the path curls uphill (**3h45min**). Look ahead, across the hillside, and you will see your way back to Rodopos. A 30-minute climb lies ahead; watch for the sporadic waymarking as you cross the hillside.

At the top of the climb there are TROUGHS and a container used as a SHEPHERDS' HUT (➏) — and more gravel road. It's quite nice to be on the flat! Walk right on the gravel, heading south, back to Rodopos. Some 45 minutes from getting onto this road and leaving the container shed, having passed pasture on the left, then animal pens and a stock shed on the right, and finally a vineyard on the left, Rodopos will be in view, with its easily-recognisable church. Stay on the gravel road and, when it becomes surfaced, go right. Then take the first left turn, up to the village square in **Rodopos** (**O**; **5h30min**).

Walk 13: A CIRCUIT FROM KOLIMBARI VIA MONI GONIA

Distance: 12km/7.5mi; 2h30min
Grade: ● straightforward; on roads and tracks, with an ascent/descent of about 200m/650ft overall
Equipment: walking trainers, sunhat, picnic, water, suitable clothing for a visit to the monastery (trousers for men and longish skirts for women). *Note:* Moni Gonia is open 08.00-12.00 and 16.00-19.00 daily except Saturday.
Picnic: at Kolimbari or Moni Gonia
Access: 🚗 or 🚌 to/from 'Kolimbari Avra' (Timetables 7, 8) or one of the frequent buses running between Kastelli-Kissamos and Hania. Park near the old port shown below (➊; 35° 32.702'N, 23° 46.774'E).

This short but interesting foray into the Cretan countryside combines the quiet attraction of hillside and coastal villages with an opportunity to visit a peaceful seaside monastery. Starting in Kolimbari, a relaxed backwater just off the national highway, within easy reach of Hania, the walk goes through the very attractive villages of Afrata and Astratigos, past and through fields, down into a valley and up again, before returning to the sea at Kolimbari.

Start the walk in **Kolimbari**: whether on foot from the 'Kolimbari Avra' bus stop or in your car, follow the sign 'AFRATA 5KM' from the main crossroads (◎). This road first passes Kolimbari's PORT (➊), where it is most convenient to leave your car.

You then pass the 17th-century Venetian fortress monastery, **Moni Gonia** (**15min**). It was an important centre for Cretan Resistance fighters during the Second World War. (When we wrote the first editions of this book, a key figure in the Resistance was running a hotel at the main crossroads under the his wartime code name, Rosmarie.)

Continue along the road as it climbs the cliff to Afrata. Compensating for the asphalt there

The harbour at Kolimbari. Take a break here at Mylos, a pleasant café in a converted mill by the water's edge, opposite the bakery/confectioners. Moni Gonia is visible in the background. Opposite: church at Astratigos

are beautiful sea views as you climb, then the route turns inland through olive groves and vineyards. In **Afrata** (**1h**) walk past the church to a small square with two *cafeneions,* a nice place to relax. Then follow signposting to the left for 'ASTRATIGOS 2KM', heading up beside a ravine which you will cross later.

Once in **Astratigos** (**1h25min**), walk past a church on your left. Leaving Astratigos you approach a sign on your right denoting the end of the village. Some 20m past this sign, take the GRAVEL TRACK (❷) on the left-hand side of the road, heading obliquely left and gently downhill. Follow it until you reach a CONCRETED SECTION (❸) at a junction. Turn left, downhill — and slightly back on yourself. The track now meanders to the valley floor through olive groves, then begins to rise out of the valley on the other side. At the first Y-fork after crossing the valley floor (❹), go left. Under 200m/yds further on, at the top of the rise — with lovely views to the sea — turn right at a T-junction (**1h45min**).

Stay on this main track, ignoring a turning left, until you come to a cross tracks, some 10 minutes later, where there is a large SHRINE on the left (❺). Go straight across, descending on concrete. Six minutes later, in amongst a rather unsightly band of houses, the track becomes road just before a junction. This is **Grimbiliana**, the heart of which is an attractive old village.

Take the first turning left; the road curves round to the right and comes to a junction with another road. Turn left and head down towards the sea (❻). When you come to a Y-fork between the houses of **Kolimbari** (❼; **2h20min**), almost at sea level, keep right, into the middle of the village. Before heading right, back to the bus stop at the start of the village, turn left and, after 150m/yds, turn down to the HARBOUR (❶) to pick up your car. If you came by bus, retrace your steps to the MAIN CROSSROADS (O) and the BUS STOP (**2h30min**).

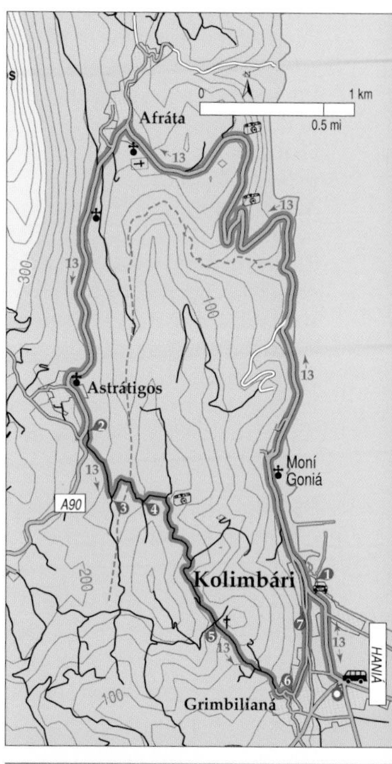

Walk 14: FROM SIRIKARI TO POLIRINIA

See also photo on page 10
Distance: 6.7km/4.2mi; 2h20min
Grade: ● straightforward; an easy gorge walk with a steep initial descent of about 300m/1000ft, then an easy gorge walk and a gentle ascent of 160m/525ft (add another 90m/295ft if you climb to the acropolis)
Equipment: walking trainers, sunhat, picnic, water
Picnic: at the rest area in the gorge or below Polirinia
Access: 🚌 to Kastelli-Kissamos (Timetable 8); journey time 45min. Change to Sirikari 🚌 (not in the timetables, but departs Mondays and Fridays *only* at 14.00 (enquire locally); journey time 1h. Return with 🚗 taxi from Polirinia to Kastelli (best to organise this before you leave Kastelli). Then 🚌 from Kastelli (Timetable 8).

Alternative walks ● Grade/equipment/access as main walk
1 Sirikari • Venetian bridge • Sirikari (6.6km/4.2mi;3h15min). 5 to Sirikari; park at the solitary church (35° 25.177'N, 23° 38.498'W). Turn back at the bridge (❷), having seen the best of the gorge.
2 Sirikari to Kastelli-Kissamos (12.5km/7.6mi; 3h30min). From the vine-covered taverna in **Polirinia** (❹), retrace your steps out of the village. After the last building on the left, descend a path left, to the road. Turn left on the road but, almost immediately, turn right on a track. Follow this all the way to Kastelli. It becomes asphalted halfway along and eventually brings you to the main road in **Kastelli** beside a supermarket. Turn left for the BUS STATION.

The Tsichliana Gorge leading to Polirinia is wide, pretty and wonderfully peaceful — filled with bright yellow Jerusalem sage in spring and crisp pink and white oleander in summer. And a bonus to this delightful walk is a visit to Kastelli, a very pleasant town where the local people are particularly charming and helpful. Taking a morning bus from Hania gives you time to wander round Kastelli, before catching your onward bus to Sirikari — a journey affording splendid views, as you wind into the heart of the countryside.

Get off the bus where it turns round just beyond **Sirikari**, by a solitary CHURCH (○). **Start out** by taking the path at the right of an INFORMATION BOARD in the church car park. You pass through a waymarked STOCK CONTROL GATE almost at once and descend quite steeply towards the gorge. When you meet a concrete track (**5min**) follow it to the right. After about 50m/yds, you come to an OLD FARMSTEAD. Weave between the buildings and bear right where the path divides.

Keep on the waymarked path along the right-hand side of the valley. The river bed is lined with leafy plane trees. Soon the route is at the beginning of the **Tsichliana Gorge**, and the air is light and fresh. About halfway along the river bed, you will pass some well-placed rustic PICNIC TABLES (❶), a good place for a break.

By **1h25min** the path has taken you well up the right-hand side of the gorge, and the landscape has opened up. Soon, another valley meets this one from the right, and the village of Polirinia can be seen ahead in the distance, its church set

The cobbled Venetian bridge

on the heights. Cross a pretty, old cobbled VENETIAN BRIDGE (❷; **1h35min**), then continue parallel with the river bed, now on your right, past some fencing.

The path soon widens into a track, passing a concrete PUMP HOUSE (❸) on the left. Walk uphill to and through a STOCK CONTROL FENCE and turn right downhill, following the track until it merges with a road coming from the right (**1h50min**). Follow this road uphill. Soon you pass the first houses of Polirinia. This is another pleasant setting for a countryside picnic (see photo on page 10). Although there are short-cut paths up through the houses, from here the most straightforward route into the village is via the road — follow it to the left uphill (keeping right at a Y-fork); then, where it meets the road Kastelli/Polirinia road, turn sharp right in a tight hairpin bend and follow it round into **Polirinia** (**2h20min**). You emerge at a small open area with a VINE-COVERED TAVERNA (❹). A taxi, or friends, could meet you here.

Otherwise, if you are still feeling energetic, we urge you to carry on with the Alternative walk to Kastelli, a very pleasant 5.5km-long downhill stroll through olive groves, with frequent views of the coast below.

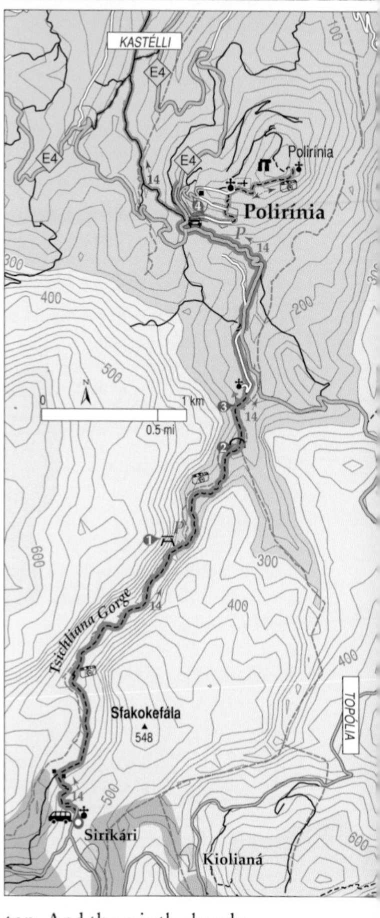

Before leaving Polirinia, take time to walk east through the village, to explore the 'ANCIENT FORTIFICATION TOWER' and AQUEDUCT (with drinking water). From the CAFENEION in another small open area in the centre of the village, you could climb the steep steps up to the CHURCH AND CEMETERY. From there a path winds up to the right, rounding the ACROPOLIS HILL. It's worth making the effort — you will have a splendid view from the top. And there is the handy Acropolis Taverna just a couple of hundred metres further west along the ridge — another place where a taxi or friends could collect you.

Walk 15: KATSOMATADOS • MOURI • VOULGARO

Distance: 11.4km/7mi; 3h20min
Grade: ● easy-moderate, with an initial ascent of about 250m/800ft, followed by a descent (sometimes a scramble) of 450m/1500ft
Equipment: walking trainers, sunhat, picnic, water
Picnic: Katsomatados, near the start of the walk
Access: Elafonisi 🚌 to Katsomatados (not in the timetables, but departs 09.00 daily; journey time 1h10min. Or 🚌 to Kastelli-Kissamos (Timetable 8); journey time 45min, then 🚌 to Katsomatados (not in the timetables, departs 10.00); journey time 20min. Or by 🚗: park in Katsomatados (35° 24.328'N, 23° 40.933'E). Return on 🚌 from Voulgaro to Kastelli (not in the timetables, departs 17.10 daily); journey time 10min, then 🚌 to Hania (Timetable 8). Do *not* rely on the return Elafonisi bus, since it may well be full and not stop. Alternatively, if you travelled by car to Katsomatados, take a 🚗 taxi from Voulgaro back to Katsomatados, to pick up your car (enquire about taxis at the first *cafeneion* you come to in Voulgaro).

Short walk: Katsomatados circuit (5.1km/3mi; 1h35min). ● Easy, with an initial ascent of about 250m/800ft, followed by a gentle descent on track. Follow the main walk to ❸, then fork left on the good track that descends back to Katsomatados via Agios Dimitrios, the church shown below.

A fine wedge of lovely and varied countryside is covered in this walk. We take you through a gorge, along a pretty chestnut tree-lined valley, into some sweeping open countryside, and finally down a ravine well used by grazing flocks of sheep and goats. There's some scrambling en route, but for the most part the walk is on well-defined track.

If you take a taxi from Kastelli-Kissamos, ask the driver at a viewpoint into into the Topolia Gorge before dropping you off at Katsomatados; otherwise you can see the gorge walls quite well from the bus.

Start the walk at the BRIDGE in **Katsomatados** (◎), near the BUS STOP and CAR PARK. Walk past the large taverna called 'Arxontas' (with rooms to rent), on the left. Go straight ahead, over a water channel, and onto a track (concreted initially).

The church of Agios Dimitrios, on the Short walk route

Pass a pretty CHURCH on the left and continue along the very pleasant, shady track. Plane trees and chestnuts, olives and oleander keep everything cool, growing along the watercourse on the left. Anywhere along here is pleasant for picnicking, in this lush green setting.

Ignore a fork to the right and then one to the left (ⓐ). (This latter crosses over the stream bed and is the return route of the Short walk and an alternative way to waypoint ❸ for those of you who are allergic to bee stings.) For the moment, if you are doing the main walk, keep the stream bed on your left. At **15min** you come to a stock control gate: leave it as you find it. The track starts to climb and, five minutes later, is concreted for about 40m/yds.

When you come to a JUNCTION (❶; **20min**), follow the track as it bends sharply to the left uphill. There may be a handwritten sign here, pointing straight ahead to 'Sasalos', and with a reference to

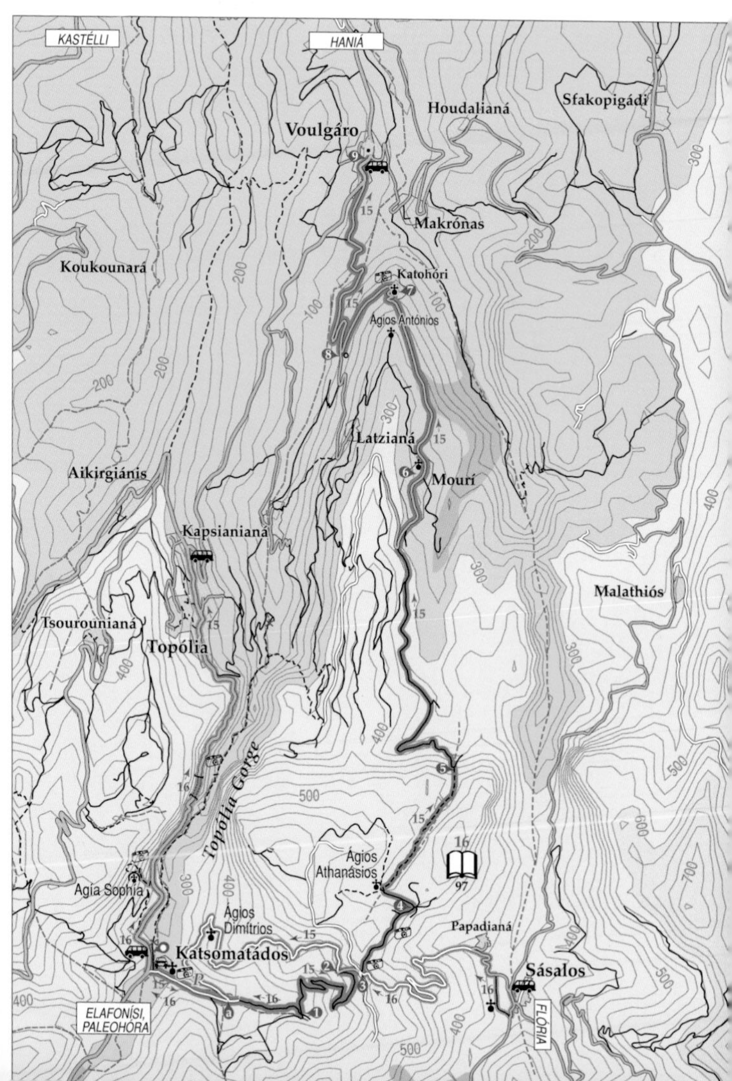

bees. *Ignore this, and be sure to bend sharp left uphill on track.* You walk out of the shade as the track becomes much wider, leading through open countryside, with gentle green hills all round. Pass a STONE SHELTER to the left and walk straight ahead on a track dotted with wooden and/or metal FEEDING TROUGHS.

It's a 30-minute climb to the top, from where there are wonderful views. Twenty minutes from the troughs you come to an intersection where the choice is a gradual right bend going downhill or a SHARP RIGHT BEND going uphill (❷): follow the follow the latter. *(But the Short walk takes the gradual right bend going downhill.)* The track acquires a concreted surface now, until reaching the SADDLE (❸; signposted in Greek to AG ATHANASIOS; **50min**), where you ignore the tracks going off right and left. Go straight ahead here

through a stock control gate secured with a piece of string. Keep on the track as it bends round to the left, ignoring a track going off sharply to the right (it leads down to Sasalos; Walk 16). A few minutes along you can see the village of Sasalos below on the right.

Eight minutes past the view over Sasalos, your track (which *may be* signposted to Agios Athanasios) forks downhill to the left (❹); ignore another track which goes straight ahead and forks. Walk between vineyards and some olive trees on the right. In five minutes you will be facing a mesh fence blocking the path to the stream bed directly in front. Make your way to the church of **Agios Athanasios** on the far bank. From here a well-defined path runs diagonally back to the stream bed. Leave via the gated fence on the far side of the church.

Once in the stream bed (**1h15min**), head north-northeast along it; a rough path leads you beside, in and over the dry water-course. Goats and sheep wander about and sit in the shade, close to the piped water running along the route. The stream bed becomes a ravine a bit further on, where the animals shelter from the sun. Walking here in spring and early summer you'll find a mass of pungent dragon lilies standing sentry, together with thick Jerusalem sage.

At **1h30min** come to a point where you can see through high, sloping rock walls to the countryside beyond. The route then starts to descend steeply, as the stream bed becomes a ravine. It's necessary to scramble in places. Keep to the left-hand side. Five minutes later, at the narrowest point, a stock control fence might bar the way: negotiate it and continue downhill, picking your own route. Within 10 minutes you emerge on a TRACK (❺) that crosses the watercourse: turn left.

In early summer you will be surrounded by bright yellow broom; in autumn the yellows and golds of vineyards lend mellow overtones to the landscape. Soon, beyond another stock control gate, keep on the main track, ignoring any turning to the left or right.

After about 30 minutes, the track — more of a dirt road by now — becomes asphalted, and you meet a fork: walk downhill to the right. Within a few minutes you will pass the first houses of **Mouri** (❻; **2h35min**), a very small village. There's an old *cafeneion* on the right, shaded by vines and mulberries. Keep ahead on the asphalt road, soon passing a CHURCH on your left.

Twenty minutes from the *cafeneion,* the road winds down into the tiny hamlet of **Katohori** (❼; **2h55min**), looping round a concrete, red-tiled CHURCH en route. Voulgaro can be seen across the valley and, a bit further on, the village of Topolia comes into view, with the narrow gorge leading to Katsomatados to its left. Just before the road eventually passes a small road off south to Latziana, you can marvel at the CHARCOAL BURNING VAT (❽) shown opposite, surrounded by wood which will go into the fire. Then the road crosses the river bed.

When you meet the main road, turn right into **Voulgaro** (O; **3h20min**). There is a bus stop before the church, but it wasn't signed at press date. Best to enquire at a *cafeneion* about buses or taxis.

Photos at the left: church in Mouri (top left), stream at the start of the walk in Katsomatados (top right) and charcoal burners' vat not far below Katohori, with cut wood ready for burning

Walk 16: SASALOS • KATSOMATADOS • TOPOLIA

See also photos on pages 1, 2, 94
Distance: 9km/5.5mi; 2h15min
Grade: ● quite easy; ascents of 200m/650ft and descents of 250m/820ft overall — ***but with a narrow, claustropobia-inducing tunnel***
Equipment: walking trainers, sunhat, picnic, water; ***good torch***
Picnic: Sasalos, Katsomatados
Access: bus to Kastelli-Kissamos (Timetable 8); journey time 45min; then bus to Sasalos (not in the timetables, departs 14.00 Tuesdays and Fridays *only;* enquire locally); journey time approximately 1h. Or Kastelli taxi to Sasalos. Return on bus from Topolia to Kastelli (not in the timetables, departs about 16.45 daily); journey time 30min; or taxi to Kastelli. Then bus to Hania (Timetable 8); journey 45min
Short walk: From Sasalos to Katsomatados (5km/3mi; 1h35min). ● Follow the main walk to Katsomatados and call for a taxi from one of the tavernas in the village or the Oasis Taverna on the main road.

Taking a straightforward route from Sasalos to Topolia, this walk makes a delightful afternoon's ramble. The countryside stays green throughout the summer, oleanders cover the hillsides, and leafy chestnut trees line and shade the country track for part of the way. Give yourselves plenty of time to wander round Kastelli-Kissamos before taking the onward bus to Sasalos.

No matter where the bus stops, **start out** by walking on into **Sasalos (○)**, passing a road off left signposted to 'FLORIA'. Then go right, over a BRIDGE and, just past a building on the right, turn right on a concrete track. Walk past an old barn-like building set back from the road and head towards a CHURCH (❶). At the church, turn right along the stream and follow the track through the trees. When you meet a road coming from the village, join it and head left uphill. In five minutes, the road bends right into the hamlet of Papadiana (❷). Go left here; the tarmac gives way immediately to a concrete and gravel track. Follow this uphill, ignoring any turn-offs.

Eventually, the track levels out (**40min**). You can see the track to Voulgaro (Walk 15) ahead, making a long bend to the right. Look for a short, steep stretch of track heading sharply back to the left and follow it uphill. Go through the stock control gate at the SADDLE on the top of the ridge (❸) and you will find yourself looking down over the fertile hills spreading out ahead into the distance. Three tracks lead off from here: take the middle one; it bends down to a valley which leads to Katsomatados.

A few minutes later (150m further on), at another fork, head left on the track that goes down towards the bottom of the valley. (Or take the track to the right, passing the chapel shown on page 92; both branches lead to Katsomatados.) Some 25 minutes from the top of the ridge, beyond some FEEDING TROUGHS and a stone ANIMAL SHELTER on the right, the track enters the tree line. Ignore a footpath signed to 'Kastanodasos' (an old chestnut wood) and follow the track as it turns down to the right and crosses the stream. Continue straight downhill, in the shade of leafy chestnuts.

Just beyond a very pretty CHURCH on the right and then a large taverna called 'Arxontas',

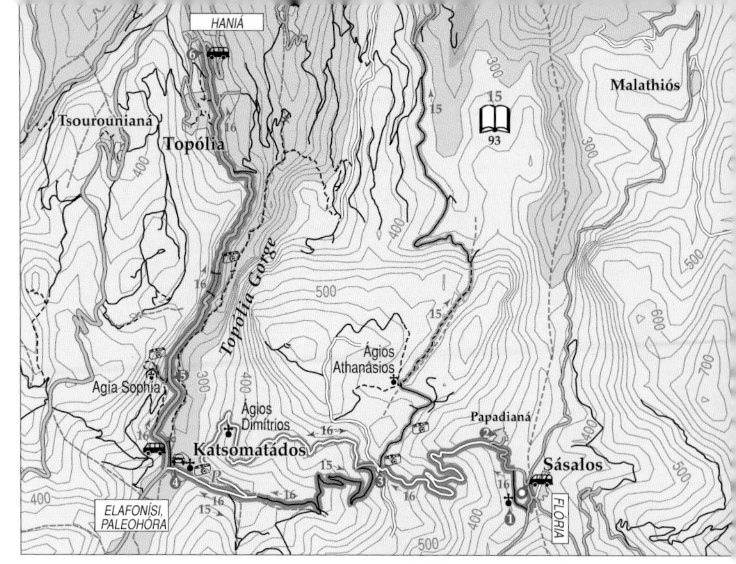

you come into **Katsomatados** (➍; **1h30min**). Continue straight ahead. Cross the BRIDGE over the river bed and bend left with the concrete track, up onto the main asphalt road. Turn right here and follow this road all the way Topolia, 40 minutes away (the gorge itself is gated off). Some 300m along there's a pleasant taverna on the right called OASIS.

Soon you see a tunnel cutting into the wall of the **Topolia Gorge**. A few minutes before the tunnel entrance, a sign indicates AGIA SOPHIA (➎; Αγ Σοφια). This tiny church, shown on the title page, is built inside a cave with stalactites and stalagmites — just a 10-minute climb off the road (a star at the top of the church, just visible at the mouth of the cave, can be seen from the road.

Having made the effort to climb up … or not, continue along the main road, negotiating the very dark, narrow 150 metre-long TUNNEL carefully and ***waving your torch so any motorists know you are there.*** The Topolia Gorge runs deep to the right of the road. About 200m/yds after exiting the tunnel, you can admire the view from a small *cantina* overlooking the gorge.

Sasalos church, near the start of the walk

When you arrive at **Topolia** (**2h15min**) hail a passing taxi … perhaps after spending some time taking photos of (or buying) some things on sale at the wonderfully eccentric 'local workshop'. There are usually taxis parked somewhere on the main road in this top part of the village. Or, if you started the walk early (perhaps had a lift), you may be in time for the 15.30 bus. There's a BUS SHELTER ahead, just before the road hairpins to the right, signposted to 'HANIA 40KM' (➏).

Walk 17: THE AGIA IRINI GORGE

See also photo on page 24
Distance: 12km/7.4mi; 3h30min
Grade: ● straightforward gorge walk descending about 600m/2000ft; waymarked. Some short steep sections require agility. Plenty of shade except for the final 2.5km along the road to Sougia (this can be avoided from May-October, when a bus leaves for Sougia from the car park at the end of the gorge).
Equipment: walking trainers, sunhat, picnic, water, swimwear
Picnic: at the gorge rest areas, with tables, fountains, WCs
Access: Sougia 🚌 (Timetable 6); ask to get off at the Irini Gorge ('fah-**rah**-gee') itself, or at Agia Irini (then walk south downhill for 10min to the gorge) or at Epanohori (then walk 7min north uphill to the gorge); journey time 1h15min. Return on 🚌 from Sougia (Timetable 6); journey time 1h30min
Note: there is a small fee to enter the gorge.

The Agia Irini Gorge has been made easily passable by mechanics and man, perhaps to take some pressure off the Samaria Gorge — and perhaps to make another tourist haunt! Although there are seating areas and drinking water is available, the gorge is still very much in its natural state. Although not as dramatic as Samaria, Irini makes a good walk most of the year, and Sougia is a pleasant, somewhat sleepy, backwater at which to end up and have a swim before the return. You could even stay overnight there, walk via Lisos to Paleohora the next day (Walk 17) or even carry on from Paleohora to Elafonisi (Walk 18) and get a bus back to Hania from there.

Start the walk on the road to Sougia, by the SIGNBOARD (○) for the gorge; follow the track down to a taverna (with parking), then the ticket kiosk (with WC). Now the stream bed starts on your left. Pines scent the air, and chestnut trees provide leafy cover as you approach the **Agia Irini Gorge**. In seven minutes the track crosses the stream bed and before long becomes a path, as it rises above the stream bed again.

From now on it is straightforward waymarked walking, with several REST AREAS (❶-❹) and other 'unofficial' places to picnic surrounded by massive rockfalls and grandiose scenery.

By **2h30min** you will be aware that the gorge is ending, as you look ahead to hillsides. When there are olive groves on either side of you (**2h40min**), the waymarked route heads uphill, out of the river bed (❺). Turn left on an asphalt road just beyond a SNACK BAR. Following the river bed on your right, you eventually come to a large car park. Up to the left is a CHURCH, and down to the right an old Venetian BRIDGE (❻), in the middle of the river bed.

Continue downhill, join another road, and turn right over a BRIDGE (❼; just over **3h**). Soon the road rises to the main Sougia road: turn left and walk the last 2.5km to **Sougia** (○; **3h30min**).

Photo: In the Agia Irini Gorge

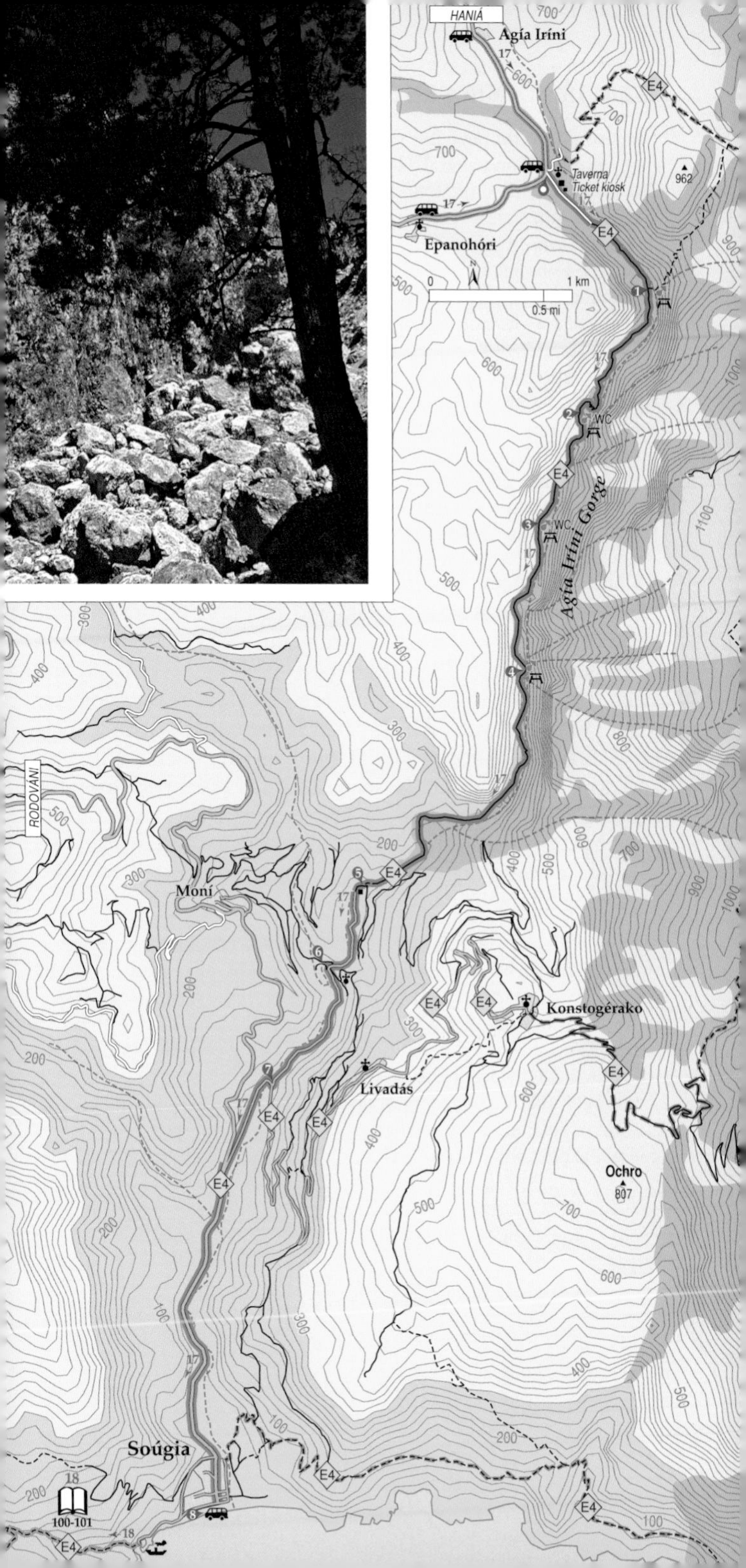
HANIÁ
Agía Iríni
Taverna
Ticket kiosk
Epanohóri
0
1 km
0.5 mi
962
Agia Irini Gorge
WC
WC
RODOVANI
Moní
Konstogérako
Livadás
Ochro
807
Soúgia
100-101
E4
17
18

Walk 18: SOUGIA • LISOS • PALEOHORA

See also photo on page 24; the map continues on pages 102-103
Distance: 15km/9.3mi; 4h45min
Grade: ● moderate-strenuous, with ups and downs of 400m/1300ft overall; E4 waymarked
Equipment: walking trainers, sunhat, long socks/trousers, picnic, ample water
Picnic: in the gorge or at the site
Access: 🚌 to Sougia (Timetable 6); journey time 1h30min. Return on 🚌 from Paleohora (Timetable 5); journey time 2h
Short walk: Sougia — Lisos — Sougia (8km/5mi; 2h30min). ● Moderate climb and descent of 150m/500ft; equipment as main walk. 🚌 to/from Sougia (Timetable 6); journey time 1h30min. Or 🚗 (35° 14.919'N, 23° 48.707'E).
Alternative walk: Sougia circuit (6.3km/3.9mi; 2h15min). ● Grade/equipment/access as *Short walk* (ups/downs of 250m/820ft). Follow the main walk for 30 minutes, then *leave* the E4 at the sign 'SOUGIA ROUND WALK' (➊) and refer to the map. *Orientation skills* needed from leaving the gorge until you join the TRACK at ➐; *watch carefully* for the sparse red dot/cairn waymarking.

The bus ride to Sougia, where this walk starts, is through a picturesque wooded valley and tree-clad hillsides — the western foothills of the White Mountains — glorious in autumn colours. The bus follows the Agia Irini Gorge (Walk 16) and river bed down to the Libyan Sea. This sea is ever in view throughout the walk, which parallels the coast. The first stage takes us through an exceedingly pretty gorge, then uphill, over, and down to the ancient Roman site at Lisos, set back from the sheltered bay of Agios Kyrkos. The second pull brings us up and across a large, flat-topped headland, before we head back down to the sea and along a length of coast, punctuated by bays, stretching all the way to Paleohora.

The bus will drop you beside a sweep of shingle beach in **Sougia**. Facing the sea, **start off** by heading right (west) from the BUS STOP/CAR PARKS (⓪). Keep round to the right when the road divides at Sougia's small HARBOUR. A rock face rears up in front of you, and a sign points you in the direction of 'LISOS'. The path is plentifully E4-waymarked (one might say obtrusively so) and leads into the very pretty gorge shown opposite, thick with brilliant pink oleander in late spring and summer. Choose your picnic spot — under carobs, olives or pines, in the gorge or beside it.

Just **25min** into the walk, the

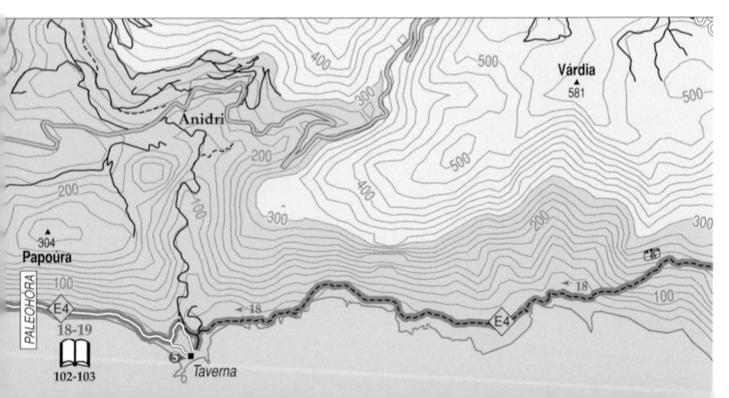

smooth gorge walls tower up above you. Five minutes later, be sure to follow the E4 path up to the left, *leaving* the gorge (❶; **30min**). *(The Alternative walk keeps straight on.)*

Some **50min** into the walk you will see Lisos below you, set back from its lovely sheltered bay. The path twists downhill; you pass the mouth of a CAVE (❷; **1h**) up to the right. **Lisos** is reached in about **1h15min**. If the site isn't open, look for the keeper, who can usually be found in his nearby house that doubles up as a REFRESHMENT HUT (or you can open the 'GATE' in the fencing; ❸). *(The Short walk returns from here to Sougia.)* From here follow waymarking to the west of the keeper's house, just above a THRESHING FLOOR.

Where a DIRT ROAD (❹) eventually cuts across your route, cross over, initially on a track. In under **2h** you should be well within sight of the south coast and your destination. There are some lovely coves in which to swim and enjoy the solitude. By **3h35min** you come upon a long sweep of beach, no doubt dotted with holidaymakers getting an all-over tan. This is south of Anidri, and there is a welcoming TAVERNA (❺) as well.

Just over an hour later you will be in **Paleohora** (**4h45min**). You pass the CEMETERY on your right as you come in: 200m/yds past its gate, turn right. Then take the second left, on the main street. The BUS STATION (❻) is just ahead to your left.

The gorge at Sougia (top) and the keeper's house and spring at Lisos

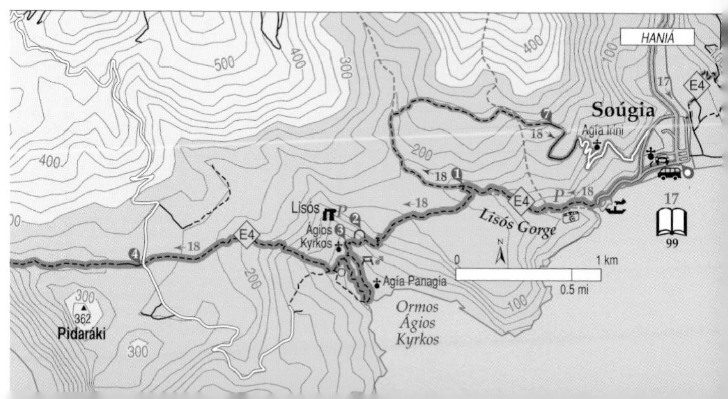

Walk 19: FROM PALEOHORA (KRIOS BEACH) TO ELAFONISI

See also photograph pages 18-19
Distance: 9.5km/5.9mi; 3h30min
Grade: moderate, with ups and downs of about 300m/1000ft overall, but you must be sure-footed and agile, with a head for heights (danger of vertigo). E4 waymarked
Equipment walking trainers, sunhat, picnic, ample water
Picnic: anywhere en route, but there's little shade except at Elafonisi

Access: to Paleohora (Timetable 5); journey time 2h (or walk from Sougia; Walk 18); then taxi to Krios Beach (7km). Return on from Elafonisi at 16.00 or from Moni Chrisoskalitisas at 18.00 (not in the timetables; *in high summer only*). Or back to Paleohora; departs 16.00, 18.00 *in high summer only*

This is a lovely coastal walk, with the sound of the sea accompanying you all the way. Paleohora is a pleasant place to stay — or spend the night if you've walked from Sougia (Walk 18). It has a good bookshop and several tavernas and café-bars where walkers congretate. From Elafonisi, you could walk 5km

An E4 waymarking pole marks the start of the walk at a small rock outcrop above Krios Beach.

to Moni Chrisoskalitisas (shown in the photograph on page 18), visit it, then catch the later (high summer only) bus to Hania from there.

The taxi will drop you by a CANTINA (◎) at the edge of **Krios Beach**. Leaving the cantina on your right (and *ignoring* two tracks to a chapel almost directly above), **start out** by heading west across the beach towards the headland, where you clamber over a small rock outcrop by the first E4 waymark post. Then take the rocky path up the hillside — marked with yellow E4 waymarks and some old red marking.

Some **10min** along, the path rises to a TRACK (❶) at the top of the first headland. Looking back beyond the beach from here, there's the sad sight of acres of plastic greenhouses — all too common along the south coast of Crete — and an unsightly contrast to the lovely sea. As the Elafonisi Peninsula comes into view in the distance, this track forks repeatedly. Keep heading in the same direction, then take the cairned fork that leads down into a rocky cove (❷).

At **1h** the path crosses quite loose scree, and there is no protection from the drops down to the sea — a vertiginous section. Ten minutes later, having crossed another ridge, the chapel of **Agios Ioannis** (❸) comes into sight. Outside it, there is a huge, inviting bell to ring; there is also a SIGNPOSTED SPRING 50m away.

If you find it hard to spot the next E4 sign, look for a cairn or old red waymark. Another vertiginous section is encountered at **1h40min**. Five minutes later the route *seems* to head uphill, away from the edge of the cliff, but walk to the edge: you may be alarmed to see an E4 sign *below* you. There is a way down! It requires some ten minutes' careful scrambling down onto a beach. Cairns and red waymarks mark the way across the beach.

Waymarking from here on is sporadic, but your direction is clear. If you're taking the BOAT back to Paleohora, you will see it moored, on its own, off the rocks to your left; a small sign indicates departure times. Beyond are the **Elafonisi** beaches shown on pages 18-19 and cantinas. The Hania BUS leaves from behind the last cantina you reach (❺; **3h30min**).

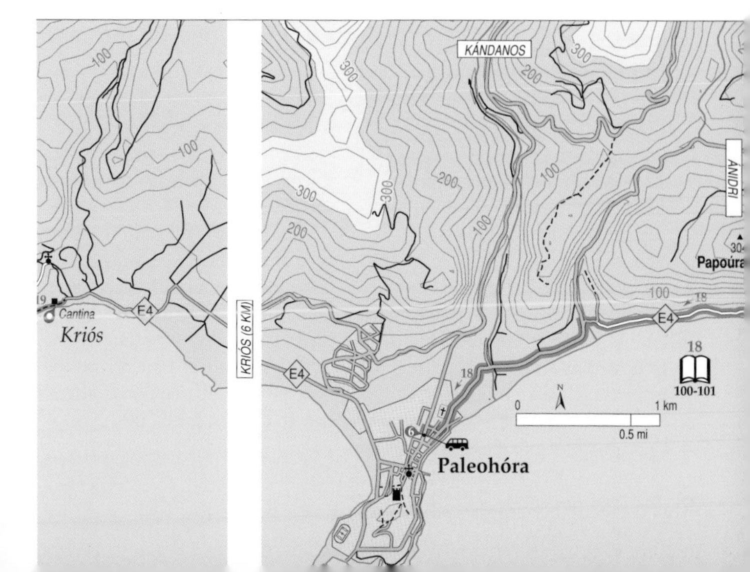

Walk 20: XILOSKALA • AFHENAS COL • GINGILOS • XILOSKALA

See also photos on pages 22-23 and 109
Distance: 9.8km/6mi; 5-6h (14.8km/7h including Volakias)
Grade: ●! very strenuous climb and descent of 1000m/3300ft overall (1150m/3770 including Volakias); you must be sure-footed with a head for heights *(danger of vertigo)*; little shade en route. E4 waymarking initially
Equipment: walking boots, windproof, sunhat, sun protection, picnic, ample water
Picnic: best shade is at the start
Access: 🚌 to/from Omalos (Timetable 3); journey time about 45min (Xiloskala is the last stop, at the top of the Samaria Gorge). In the summer season (May to October) there are more buses returning than are shown in the timetables. Or 🚗 (35° 18.495'N, 23° 55.091'E).

***Shorter walk*: Xiloskala — Afhenas Col — Xiloskala** (7.4km/4.6mi; 3h30min); equipment, access/return as main walk. Grade: ● half the climb and descent (500m/1650ft). Follow the main walk to ❹ (1h55min) and return the same way. Or go only as far as the **Linoseli Spring** at ❸ (1h20min).

By climbing Gingilos you can totally immerse yourself in the deep solitude, silence, echoes and majesty characteristic of high mountain walks. Gingilos is a magnificent and awesome mass, towering to one side of the Samaria Gorge. Wild rock formations, a massive band of scree, echoing stone walls, wild flowers clinging perilously to ledges, contorted, windswept trees, and breathtaking views are just some of this walk's delights.

Walking to the Afhenas Col (the Shorter walk) will probably be more than enough of an experience for some of you, while for others — intrepid types — you can clamber to the top of Volakias. The main walk is easier than it looks when you stand and contemplate the mountain; at 1974m/6475ft (you'll see differing heights on different maps), Gingilos may not be the highest peak on Crete, but it's certainly one of the most inspiring.

The bus turns round at the **Xiloskala** CAR PARK (◉), the top of the walk down into the Samaria Gorge (Walk 22; Walk 21 also begins here). Facing the wooden railings at the top of the *xiloskala* (Greek for 'wooden staircase'), look right, up towards a TAVERNA perched on the hillside, off the road. Our hike starts behind it. **Set off** up the path indicated by an E4 sign, passing the taverna. The path, initially with wooden railings, climbs steeply, so you gain height rapidly. Occasional trees at the side of the path give shade for pauses — and an early picnic break (there is very little shade further on).

By the time the path flattens out you are heading well away from the Omalos, which is fast receding behind you. Looking back from here gives you an excellent view of the refuge high up at Kallergi, on the far side of the Samaria Gorge (there's a photo of it on page 109). Notice

Dramatic rock formations characterise this exhilarating hike as here at the Xepitiras Arch.

two paths in particular: one in the foreground comes down to Xiloskala (Walk 21); the other, in the middle distance (to the right of Kallergi) leads through the conservation area into the Samaria Gorge (Walk 22). Where the path begins to run high on a narrow ledge — and there is a fair drop to the left side (❶; **45min**) vertigo sufferers may feel anxious.

Our path now takes us under the huge **Xeptiras Arch** shown above (❷; **50min**); Cretan ebony hangs gracefully from this rock arch, and you cannot fail to feel as though you're in the very heart of the mountains here. There are massive, dramatic rock faces, peaks, boulders and formations all around, as the photograph above shows.

At **1h15min** into the walk you

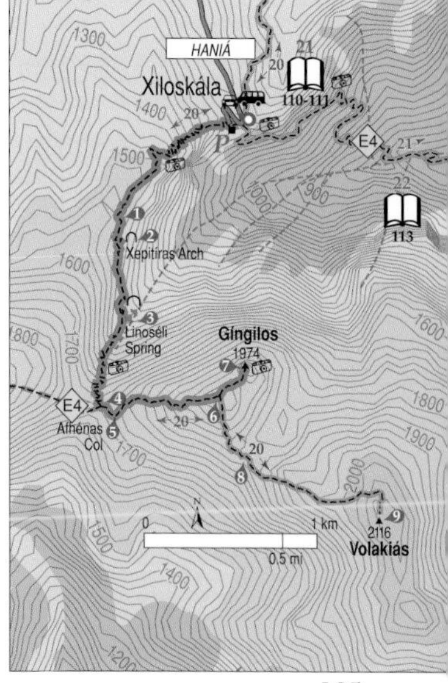

round a very large overhanging rock on the right; you will notice a CAVE SHELTER beneath it. Five minutes later, the route leads to the **Linoseli Spring** (❸; **1h20min**), where there are two troughs and an overflow pipe. From the spring the yellow-waymarked path continues up towards a MASSIVE SCREE SLOPE and a very obvious peak beyond it, pointing up into the sky. The route zigzags up over a firm scree base, and there are cairns en route as well. Some 18 minutes past the spring, the path flattens out for a short distance. A large rock offers some shade.

Eventually you will reach the **Afhenas Col** (❹; **1h55min**). Here it may well be very windy indeed, but the thrill of being up so high and seeing for miles and miles is terrific. On a clear day, looking back to Kallergi, you might just be able to pick out Theodorou Island to the left of the refuge, off the distant north coast. *(The Shorter walk turns back from here, and the E4 leaves us too, to head west and eventually south to Sougia.)*

The climb to the Gingilos summit starts from this ridge. Look left to find an arrow pointing up the edge of the mountain. Follow the yellow waymarking — do not lose sight of it — and it will lead you steeply upwards. In places it is necessary to clamber and scramble; you need to be very surefooted and confident. ***Caution:*** After about 100m/yds there is a SHEER-SIDED PIT (❺) just to the right below the marked path — it's about 2.5m/8ft in diameter and it plummets 115m/375ft straight down! It is marked off with a few iron stakes, but *beware — especially on the descent!*

Before long you will have a simply splendid view over the Omalos again and, by **2h25min**, the route will become easier as you near the top. Soon you will almost be at the top of this magnificent mountain, by a LARGE CAIRN ON A FLAT AREA (❻).* Although this *feels* like 'the top', go left here, *carefully,* to the marginally higher SUMMIT OF **Gingilos** (**2h55min**), marked by a METAL ROD (the remains of a cross) and a SHRINE.

When you have taken in the tremendous view, make your way back to the Afhenas Col by carefully following the waymarking from the large cairn on the flat. It offers a choice of routes, some easier than others. Use your discretion, knowing where you are heading. Fifty minutes later you will be back at the ridge. It's pleasant, on the way down, to be able to pay more attention to the spectacular landscape and the trees — among them the pretty Montpelier maple. It takes about 2h30min to descend back to **Xiloskala** (**5-6h**). Sit down by the café/shop in the CAR PARK (❍), so you are near where the bus turns round (rapidly) and leaves almost immediately.

---

*If you plan to continue to Volakias, walk downhill slightly from this CAIRN, heading south, and traverse to the next SADDLE (❽), from where you have another ascent of 250m/820ft to the Volakias summit, 45 minutes from Gingilos. From the saddle work your way *carefully* round the *left side* of the obvious ridge of outcropping rocks (there are some small CAIRN WAYMARKERS). (In mountaineering circles up here, Gingilos is considered 'superior' to the higher peak of **Volakias** (❾), so don't feel the *need* to press on!)

Left: at the Xiloskala

Walk 21: A HIGH MOUNTAIN CIRCUIT FROM KALLERGI

See also photos on pages 22-23 and 106
Distance: 12km/7.4mi; 6h45min (19km/12mi from/ back to Xiloskala)
Grade: ● for experienced hill-walkers: strenuous, with overall ascents/descents of about 700m/ 2300ft. Almost no shade. Partly along the E4 trail
Equipment: walking books, windproof, sunhat, scarf, GPS or compass, picnic, ample water
Picnic: near Kallergi or the Poria (meagre shade)
Access: 🚘 4WD vehicle (preferably) to/from Kallergi (35° 19.287'N, 23° 55.900'E), or stay overnight there (see under 'Short walk', page 111). Alternatively, 🚘 or 🚌 to/from Xiloskala (see Walk 20, page 104), then walk to and from Kallergi (add 320m/1050ft of ascent and 3h10min; see Short walk on page 111). This option should only be undertaken by very fit walkers.
Short walk: Xiloskala — Kallergi — Xiloskala (6.8km/4.2mi; 3h10min). ● Although mostly on a gravel track, it's quite a pull up (ascent of 320m/ 1050ft). Walking trainers, sunhat, picnic, water. Access/return: as Walk 20, page 104. See notes on page 111.

A breathtaking hike in more ways than one, the trek to Melindaou is, without doubt, worth the effort. The lure of the high mountains is a compelling experience, and this walk — in the heart of the splendid Levka Ori (White Mountains) — is an exciting introduction to high mountain walking on Crete. This expedition requires stamina. You must also be sure-footed and know how to use a compass or GPS competently. The rewards are ample, and walking in this area, we are sure, will mean the beginning of a long association with Crete's mountains. You will carry the views with you forever — the space, the fold upon fold of rock and mountainside, the colours and textures, the height, depth and strength of Western Crete.

Before setting off, be sure to tell someone at Kallergi where you are going. Then **start out**: walk the length of the southern, front side of the **Kallergi** REFUGE (◉) and follow the short path leading to a gravel track. This track heads off east towards the mountains. You will

The walker is a mere dot in the landscape on this high mountain walk which circles Mavri (the central peak). Melindaou is to the right.

The Kallergi refuge sits in a splendid position, looking out to Gingilos (Walk 19) and the White Mountains; below these heights, the Samaria Gorge slices its way to the sea.

follow it to the Poria ('Shepherds' Saddle') along the well-marked E4 route. The E4 cuts the first bend off the track by descending a stepped path on the right about 400m from Kallergi. When you rejoin the gravel track, be aware that it is also used by cross-country bikers travelling at speed. The route affords a tremendous view of Kallergi and Gingilos — as you can see in the photo above.

Some **25min** from Kallergi, when the hut is completely out of sight, and the valley falls away to the left of the track, you will have a wonderful view of mountains ... and still more mountains. From here, on a clear day, it is possible to see all the way to Theodorou Island off the north coast, west of Hania. Then (**45min**), for a good view of Gingilos and Volakias, go right off the track (at a break in the fence).

In under **1h** from Kallergi, rounding a bend in the track, you will be at a SADDLE (❶), called '**Poria**' by the shepherds. Leave the track here, and head right on the well-waymarked path (there is a building up to the right). After 50 minutes of climbing, much of which is steep, the route flattens out briefly; you will be level with the refuge, now far in the distance. This respite doesn't last long, however, and the route continues on and up, beyond a substantial CAIRN.

Fifteen minutes later, reach the top of the first ridge, from where you can feast your eyes upon yet more splendid mountains and the inspiring Cretan landscape. Head left along the ridge in a northeasterly direction and follow the waymarking. As the route rises again, *follow the waymarking assiduously.* Ten minutes later you will be on the SUMMIT OF **Psari** (❷; **2h**), marked by a short CONCRETE PILLAR with bits of iron protruding from it. From this point you can see the route leading across towards Mavri (the photograph opposite was taken here and shows the route clearly).

Setting off from the concrete pillar, continue north-northeast. In just under 10 minutes, start to climb again. Fifteen minutes later, CAIRNS mark the way, as the route skirts round to the right of **Mavri** (❸), below the summit. At **2h40min**, having gone halfway along the next ridge, notice the path heading sharply back to the left, round the

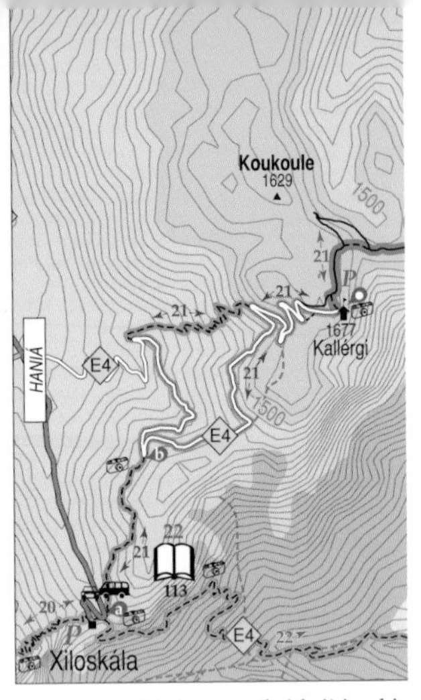

You're very likely to see 'kri kri' in this area — wild mountain goats. The refuge provides an authentic retreat from the noisy world we live in and offers simple, clean, comfortable accommodation and facilities, with an evening meal and breakfast. To book, see details under 'Short walk' opposite.

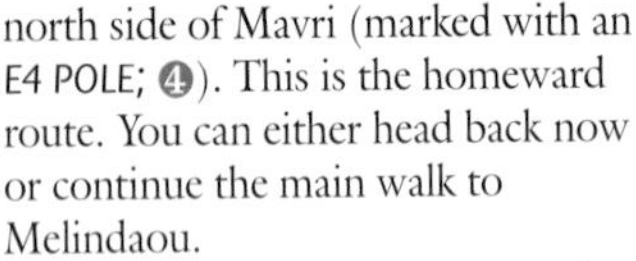

north side of Mavri (marked with an E4 POLE; ❹). This is the homeward route. You can either head back now or continue the main walk to Melindaou.

Ten minutes before the summit the walk flattens out — and then you're there! E4 poles lead you across the southern slope and you can leave the main E4 path and head diagonally up to the SUMMIT OF **Melindaou** (❺; **3h20min**).

While the E4 continues past Melindaou, there is no obvious point of return for day-walkers; the path leads on even further into the White Mountains, to Pahnes, the highest peak in the range — a couple of days' and nights' trek away. So unless you're with a guide, it's best to return to the homeward path, which you identified after passing Mavri.

From the E4 POLE (❹) it cuts a route lower down and back across the north side of the mountain, in the direction of Kallergi. Follow the waymarking poles over a ridge and look down to the right, along the valley ahead: you will spot a clear path. Pick your way carefully down towards the path and the valley floor — a rough descent lasting 15 minutes. Take care to steer clear of any beehives if you're walking here in summer.

Once on the floor of the valley, more E4 waymarking will guide you back to your outgoing track, not far from the point where you started up the mountainside. In April and May the valley floor is swathed in crocuses and wildflowers — a heartening sight for the trek back to

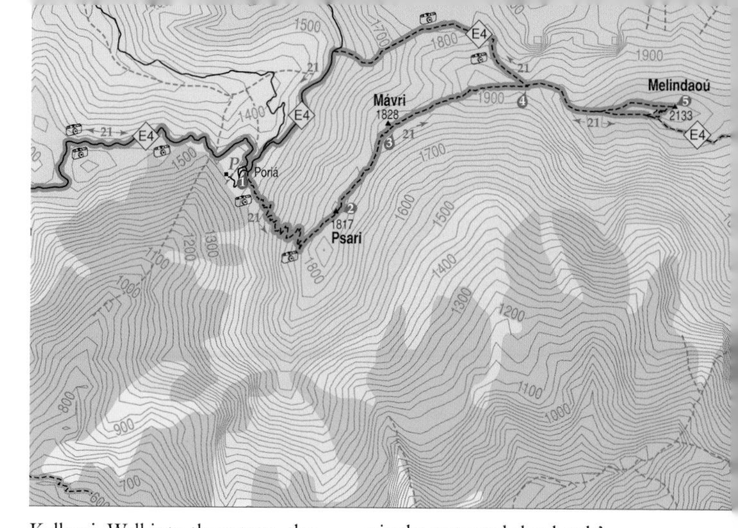

Kallergi. Well into the return, the path crosses a dried-up watercourse and continues unevenly all the way back to the track. Turn left and walk via the scattered shepherds' dwellings at the **Poria** (❶) back to **Kallergi** (O; **6h45min**); the sense of achievement is terrific.

Short walk (to Kallergi)

Kallergi is the mountain refuge in the Levka Ori that hikers and climbers use as a base for exploring the range, under the guidance and supervision of the refuge's professional Austrian management. However, you don't have to be an expert to enjoy its spectacular position, perched like an eyrie at 1677m/5470ft above sea level. You can spend a night by booking ahead (tel: 306976 585849; www.kallergi.co) — or simply visit to marvel at the views, enjoy a picnic and revel in the peaceful atmosphere of the mountains.

The path to Kallergi is marked from the CAR PARK at **Xiloskala** (ⓐ) by an INFORMATION BOARD at the left of the entrance to the Samaria Gorge. Follow the red arrow, immediately going through a GATE. The path crosses the hillside diagonally, climbing very gradually at first and running almost parallel with the car park and road below. Look back across the car park and beyond the tourist pavilion, to Gingilos, the impressive grey mass in the background. As the path rounds the shoulder of the hill, the Omalos comes into view, spread out like a tablecloth far below.

Continue on the path until it meets a rough gravel track on a hairpin bend (ⓑ; **40min**). A small cairn marks the junction; this waymarker is a help on the return. Go through the stock control fence and follow the track uphill to the right. (Ten minutes up the track, at the first big left-hand bend, the adventurous might like to follow the blue waymarking up the ravine. This scramble requires care, is no faster than the track route, and is *not* recommended as a descent.)

Just before the track reaches the top, there is a shrine, an igloo-shaped stone SHEPHERDS' SHELTER and the beginning of E4 POLE WAYMARKING. The track divides at this shelter; take the right-hand fork and walk a further 150m/yds to the **Kallergi** refuge (O), reached in **1h45min**.

Return the same way.

Walk 22: THE SAMARIA GORGE

See also photographs on pages 22-23, 106, 109 and the cover
Distance: 15km/9.3mi; 4-6h
Open: April/May to October (depending on rainfall); there is a charge to enter; pick up an English leaflet on payment.
Important note: Do not try to find an alternative route to the sea; stay on the designated path through the gorge. *This is imperative.* Swimming in the rock pools is forbidden; console yourself with the thought of a swim at the end of the walk.
Grade: ● straightforward but strenuous, particularly if you are not used to walking; the descent is 1250m/4100ft. You must be sure-footed crossing the river bed on slippery stones. Plenty of shade in the upper gorge, but full sun for the last half hour.
Equipment: walking trainers or walking boots, sunhat, water bottle (for collecting spring water), picnic, swimming things
Picnic: throughout the gorge
Access: 🚌 to Omalos (Timetable 3); journey time about 45min (get off at the last stop, Xiloskala). Return by ⛴ to Hora Sfakion, departs Agia Roumeli 15.45, 16.30, 17.00, 17.45; voyage time 1h30min. Then 🚌 from Hora Sfakion (Timetable 4); journey time about 2h

The Samaria Gorge may be one of the reasons why you have come to Crete. Even if it isn't, you will soon hear tell of it; few people can resist the lure of Europe's longest gorge. And you won't be disappointed if you can see through the people! Setting out *very* early (the gorge opens at 6am) is the best way to avoid the crowds. Although this walk follows a well-trodden path, walking the gorge requires stamina, and *robust footwear is essential*.

Enough about caution. Here's some scene-setting: the landscape is simply spectacular, from the top of the gorge at Omalos to the bottom at Agia Roumeli — and all along the south coast on your boat trip to Hora Sfakion (where you'll find your bus back to Hania and the north coast). The White Mountains tower around you as the route leads seawards under shady pine trees through which sunlight slants. You'll pass cool pools and cross wide-open stretches of ancient, bleached rocky river bed.

Imagine light and shadow; height and depth; rock in shades of grey, green, blue and brown; mountains, trees and sky; birdsong and silence. It's a special experience walking through this natural wonder. If you walk the gorge in springtime, the wild flowers are another bonus to the excursion. At whatever time of year you walk the gorge, don't go down helter-skelter, trying to beat any records. Go at a leisurely pace and take in your surroundings. We haven't given any times for reaching specific points on the walk for this very reason. Enjoy the day.

Right: the Sideroportes, where the gorge is at its most narrow

HANIÁ
110-111
Xilóskala
Neroutsiko rest area
Riza Sikias rest area
WC
Ágios Nikólaos
Vrísi rest area
E4
0
1 km
0.5 mi
Gíngilos
1974
105
Samariá rest area
Ágios Geórgios
Óssia María
Samariá
Samariá Gorge
Nero tis Perdíkas rest area
Afendis Christós
Christós rest area
Sideroportes
Checkpoint
Agía Paraskeví
Pálaia Agía Rouméli
Agía Triáda
SOÚGIA
Agía Rouméli
116-117

The bus drops you in the **Samaria Gorge** CAR PARK (⭘), by shops and a *cafeneion* with a WC, where you can 'regroup' before starting out. Then buy your ticket — and hang on to it. Half will be taken from you at the end of the gorge; it helps wardens to ascertain if everyone has gone through the gorge at the end of the day and, of course, it aids 'statistics'.

Start the walk on the **Xiloskala**, the wooden staircase down into the gorge — a solid construction made of tree trunks. Doubtless there will be a mass of other people setting off with you (up to 3000 people *a day* walk Samaria in high summer), which isn't encouraging, but the crowd thins out as people either turn back or establish their individual pace and walk and stop and walk again, marvelling at this splendid achievement of nature.

The first eye-catcher is Gingilos Mountain (see photograph on page 109) — a huge wall of rock towering majestically up to the right. You may well have already climbed Gingilos (Walk 20); it's a tremendous feeling to see the mountain from down here, particularly if you have been to the top ...

The staircase becomes a path and drops very steeply about 600m (almost 2000ft) to the bottom of the upper gorge. There are ample SPRINGS, TABLES, and WCs en route (see map), so picnicking possibilities abound. Once you've passed the small chapel of **Agios Nikolaos** (➊), nestling amongst pines and cypresses to the right, the route becomes less steep.

When you reach the **Samaria rest area** (➋) and the old hamlet of **Samaria** (➌), you will be about halfway to the sea. One of the buildings (into which you can go and sign the VISITORS' BOOK) has been restored for the wardens who replaced the original inhabitants when the gorge was designated a national park.

From Samaria, continue on towards the sea, past the **Ossia Maria** church. The path twists and turns in places, allowing for rock formations and geological contortion, crossing the watercourse by stepping-stones in some places. You will know when you reach the famous **Sideroportes** (➍; 'Iron Gates', clearly shown in the photo on page 113) — where the gorge is at its narrowest. You're at about 150m/500ft here, with rock walls soaring hundreds of metres above you on either side. Beyond this point the scenery opens out.

There are TICKET COLLECTORS and refreshment KIOSKS (➎) a couple of kilometres before road comes underfoot at **Palea (Old) Agia Roumeli.** This village was abandoned due to flash flooding: the **Tarraios River** is so full in winter that the gorge has to be closed. Cross to the cemetery church of **Agia Triada**; a FERRY SHUTTLE BUS runs from here in high season. Eventually you come into **Agia Roumeli** itself (keep left at the first fork and right at the second) — perhaps somewhat weary and ready for a refreshing swim in the Libyan Sea, before taking the ferry (➏) to Hora Sfakion.

Weary or not, you will feel exhilarated beyond measure; 'walking Samaria' is an unforgettable achievement. You might even stay the night here and carry on to Loutro tomorrow (Walk 23).

Walk 23: FROM AGIA ROUMELI TO LOUTRO

Map continues on page 120
Distance: 15km/9.3mi; 5h05min
Grade: ●: moderate-strenuous, with some scrambling; ascents/descents of 300m/1000ft overall; possibility of vertigo on one short stretch. E4-waymarked
Equipment: walking trainers, sunhat, picnic, water, swimming things
Picnic: Agios Pavlos
Access: 🚌 to Hora Sfakion (Timetable 4); journey time about 2h. Then ⛴ to Agia Roumeli: departs Hora Sfakion daily at 10.30, 13.00, 16.50, 18.00; voyage time 1h30min. Return by ⛴ from Loutro to Hora Sfakion: departs daily at 09.30, 10.30, 11.30, 12.30, 13.30, 16.00, 17.00, 18.10; voyage time 30min. Then 🚌 to Hania (Timetable 4; buses connect with the boats); journey time about 2h
Alternative walks: Combine this with Walk 21, 23 or 24.

The gorgeous hike between Agia Roumeli and Hora Sfakion splits nicely into two, and that's how we describe it. But whether you undertake it as one walk or two, do start out early, to benefit from the early morning cool. The first stage of the walk has some shade, but the leg from Loutro to Hora Sfakion (Walk 25) is virtually devoid of it. High cliffs form a towering wall to the left, sometimes close at hand, edging the path, elsewhere set back in high majesty. Moving east, you will skirt

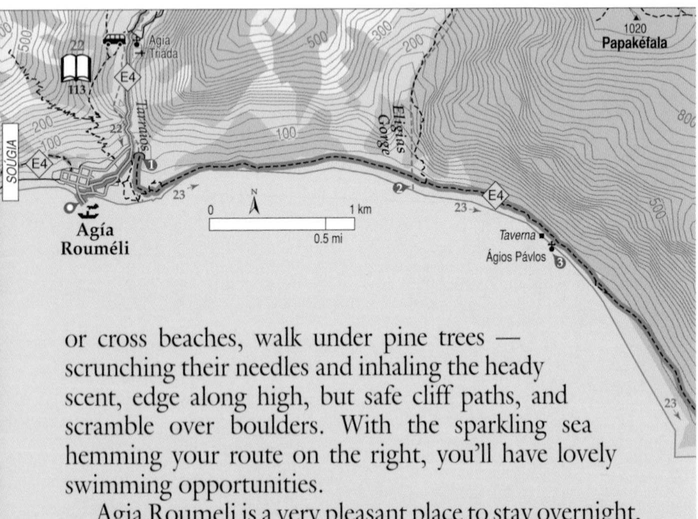

or cross beaches, walk under pine trees — scrunching their needles and inhaling the heady scent, edge along high, but safe cliff paths, and scramble over boulders. With the sparkling sea hemming your route on the right, you'll have lovely swimming opportunities.

Agia Roumeli is a very pleasant place to stay overnight, *after* the Samaria Gorge-walkers have left with the last boat. The same is true of Loutro and Lykkos (the ancient port of Finix, just west of Loutro). All have rooms for rent.

Photo: Loutro

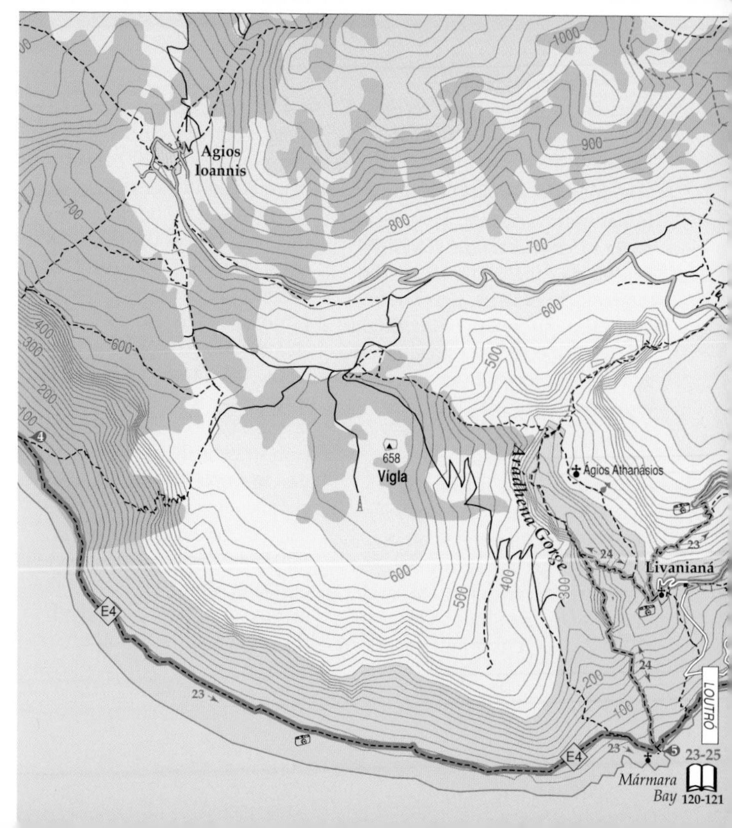
Agios
Ioannis
1000
900
800
700
600
500
400
300
200
100
658
Vígla
Arádhena Gorge
Ágios Athanásios
Livanianá
LOUTRÓ
E4
23
24
23-25
Mármara
Bay
120-121

Agios Pavlos — a lovely place to stop for a pause or a picnic

Start out from the FERRY (⓪) by walking to the middle of **Agia Roumeli**, and then towards the bottom of the **Samaria Gorge**. Either wade across the **Tarraios River** or cross it via the VENETIAN BRIDGE (❶), then continue on the WAYMARKED E4 PATH. Beyond the inconspicuous mouth of the **Eligias Gorge**, you come to a small TAVERNA and then the lovely Byzantine church of **Agios Pavlos** (❷; **1h25min**). About half an hour from this point, keep to the lower path (the upper one goes to Agios Ioannis; ❹).

In under four hours you will have a stiff pull up and scramble, before arriving at gorgeous **Marmara** (Marble) **Bay** (❺) at the mouth of the **Aradhena Gorge** (Walk 24) — perfect for a swim or a rest. Vertigo sufferers may find the going a bit testing on a short section of exposed path (**4h**) between Marmara and **Lykkos Bay** (❻).

Then you are on the last leg: the route goes across the terrace of the last TAVERNA and up steps. Once over the next hill you will be able to see Livaniana (Walk 24) up to the left and, down to the right, what used to be the ancient port of **Finix** (❼), where there is now a pleasant taverna. Continue on the waymarked path straight ahead, above Finix, to pass the VENETIAN CASTLE in its commanding position and then reach the haven of **Loutro** (❽; **5h05min**). Alternatively, round the headland from FINIX BEACH: this involves one more short climb past the castle (adds 10 minutes).

Walk 24: LOUTRO AND THE ARADHENA GORGE

See also photo on page 117
Distance: 18km/11.2mi; 7h05min
Grade: ●❢ straightforward but strenuous, with 650m/2150ft of ascents/descents, some quite steep. You must be sure-footed and have a head for heights (possibility of vertigo). Various waymarks, including E4
Equipment: walking trainers, sunhat, picnic, water, swimwear
Picnic: Aradhena Gorge (shade)
Access: 🚌 to Hora Sfakion (Timetable 4); journey time about 2h. Then ⛴ to Loutro: departs Hora Sfakion daily at 10.00, 11.00, 12.00, 13.00, 14.00, 16.30, 17.30, 18.30; voyage time 30min. Return by ⛴ from Loutro to Hora Sfakion: departs daily at 09.30, 10.30, 11.30, 12.30, 13.30, 16.00, 17.00, 18.10; voyage time 30min. Then 🚌 to Hania (Timetable 4; buses connect with the boats); journey time about 2h

Optional start: Loutro headland. ●❢ This optional way to start any of the walks adds 10 minutes. At the western end of Loutro go up steps at the left of the Hotel Daskalogiannis, signposted 'PATH TO VENETIAN CASTLE, ROMAN REMAINS'). Walk over the terrace of the Porto Loutro Hotel on the Hill and go through a gate, then continue past the Roman remains and the CHURCH AND CEMETERY to the left on the headland. Some 15min from Loutro, where a sewage CISTERN interrupts the path, continue by following the blue dots. Before long you will see Livaniana tucked up into the hillside ahead, to the right. When you arrive at **Finix Beach** (30min), head for the CHURCH WITH THE NORFOLK PINE. Go through a gate and curl up behind the church in a gentle bend, and continue west and uphill until you meet the well-waymarked E4 route.

Shorter walk: Loutro — Aradhena Gorge — Livaniana — Loutro (10km/6.2mi; 4h05min). ●❢ Grade, equipment, access/return as main walk (but only half the climbing). Follow the main walk to the junction at 2h45min, on the outskirts of **Livaniana** (❺). Instead of turning sharply left here, follow the waymarking down through the houses. There is a taverna with a tremendous view on the far side of the village — the only sign of life! Just past the taverna the track to Lykkos descends to the right. Do *not* take this, but continue for another 50m/yds, climbing a little, until you come to the old donkey trail (ⓐ) on your right, waymarked in blue. Follow this as it zigzags down to the **Finix** tavernas, then head for the CHURCH WITH THE NORFOLK PINE. Go through a gate, curl up behind the church in a gentle bend and continue uphill until you meet the E4. Now retrace your outgoing route back to **Loutro** (**O**).

Alternative walks

1 ***Combined Walks 22-25*** (requires overnight stays at Agia Roumeli and Loutro or Finix). First descend the Samaria Gorge; walk on to Loutro the next day, do this walk, then carry on to Hora Sfakion.

2 ***Loutro — Livaniana — Aradhena Gorge — Loutro*** (11km/6.8mi; 4h15min). ●❢ Grade, equipment, access/return as main walk (but ascent/descent of 350m/1150ft). This is a good choice if you want to relax at beautiful Marmara Beach at the end of the day, but the steep descent from Livaniana and down the gorge is quite taxing. Start out by walking to **Finix Beach** via the headland at Loutro (see 'Optional start' above). Beyond Finix, when you meet the waymarked E4 route (❶), cross over and continue steeply uphill to the

right. The way peters out into a path and then becomes an old blue-waymarked donkey trail zigzagging neatly uphill. There is a great view as you ascend. When you reach the outskirts of **Livaniana**, walk up onto a ROAD (ⓐ). You can rest or replenish your water supply in the small taverna on the left. Then take the waymarked zigzag path and steps up through the village. The path passes an old outdoor oven and meets the chicken wire above the village CHURCH (❺; 1h30min). Continue above the church, making for the gorge (faded blue waymarking). Head down towards terraced olive trees and, after passing between wooden gateposts, turn left. Descend steeply through more olive tree terracing until you reach the dry stream bed (❸; by a large solitary olive tree). Here the path crosses to the other side of the gorge. Make your way down through the boulder-strewn gorge (cairns and various waymarking colours) to **Marmara Beach** (3h). Then take the E4 path east to **Loutro** (O; 4h15min).

3 Loutro — Livaniana — Aradhena — Anopolis — Loutro (13km/8mi; 5h50min). ●: Grade, equipment, access/return as main walk. If you want to enjoy Marmara Beach another day (when you can either walk a short way up the Aradhena Gorge or follow the Shorter walk above), then omit the gorge. Follow ALTERNATIVE WALK 2 to the church in **Livaniana** (❺; 1h30min). Then pick up the main walk at the 2h45min-point and follow it to the end, saving 1h15min.

This is a glorious combination of coast, seaside village, gorge and mountain village, which can be done in many different ways. We prefer to walk two-thirds of the way *up* the lower gorge (enjoying the best part of it), and then come back *downhill* to Loutro via Anopolis — since this last section is long, steep and exposed. But if you stay overnight in Loutro you will no doubt

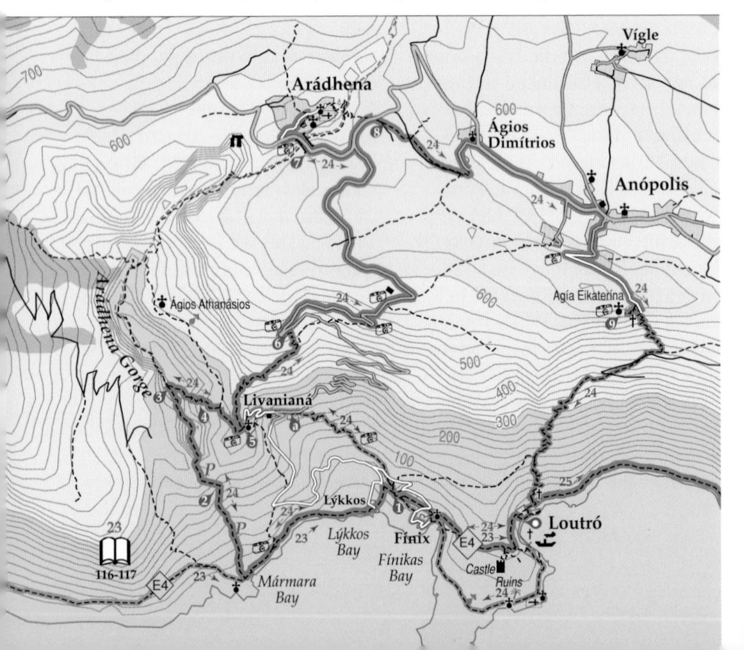

meet people who walk *up* to Anopolis, on to Aradhena, and *down the whole gorge* or vice versa. They follow a high zig-zagging path cut into the side of the upper gorge. Although this path bypasses the original steel ladders bolted to the rock face, it could still be challenging for vertigo-sufferers. Our map shows the route in detail, although we don't describe it.

Start the walk from the middle of the beach (**O**) in **Loutro**. Walk into the village, passing to the right of the KIOSK on the beach. Turn left by Sofia's mini-market, then head round to the left (blue waymarking) on the obvious path running in an arc behind the village. Pass houses on your right and walk through a gate, just after which you will see an E4 SIGN on an ancient olive tree. Ignore a turning to the left (by a SHRINE on the left). Continue winding up the path, ignoring gates to the left; follow the blue waymarking.

At a junction, where the VENETIAN CASTLE RUINS are signposted to the left, keep right for 'FINIX' on the E4 path. The path follows the wall surrounding the castle ruins and leads to the brow of the hillside. The village tucked up into the hillside ahead, to the right, is Livaniana, which you will skirt later in the walk. Soon your complete coastal route can be seen stretching out in front of you.

As you start descending, **Finix Beach** comes into view — a smattering of blue and white tavernas and rooms for rent. The route zigzags down behind them, leaving a whitewashed CHURCH WITH THE NORFOLK PINE down to the left. Just past the church, cross diagonally over a track. (Some 350m past here, at a Y-fork (**1**), Alternative walks 2 and 3 climb to Livaniana on a blue-waymarked donkey trail, and the Shorter walk descends this trail.) Continue on the well-waymarked E4 path in the general direction of the coast. Before long you are over the next small headland (where there are more tavernas with rooms to rent) and down by the sea at **Lykkos Beach** (**30min**).

Keep straight on downhill, hugging the rocks on your left. Descend amidst the line of buildings. The path heads down some concrete steps, across taverna terraces, and then across a flat pebbly stretch behind a beach. The last building en route is a restaurant. Walk along this beach to the next cove, at the far side of which there is an E4 SIGN. Here steps hewn out of the rock take you steeply up onto the cliffs (you'll have to use your hands in places). You need to *go carefully* here, as the path curls tightly up to the right, past a cave. Where the path is difficult to discern, YELLOW PAINT DAUBS identify the route. Those who suffer from vertigo will find this exposed stretch the most difficult part of the walk.

Once over the next headland you

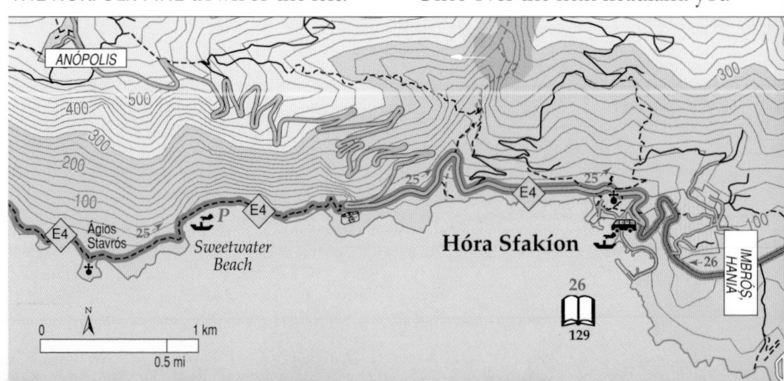

will be looking down over **Marmara** (Marble) **Beach**, beyond which are a few buildings and a small CHURCH. The path descends to a flatter area and bears left to this beach (**1h15min**) with its crystal-clear, inviting water. From here *ignore* the E4 signs, which now lead along the coast (the route of Walk 23).

Instead, head inland, following a stream bed into the mouth of the **Aradhena Gorge**. The atmosphere

Ruins at Aradhena, with a view to the White Mountains

changes rapidly as huge rock faces tower either side of the route, providing cooling shade. Five minutes into the gorge, the magnificent rock wall on your right has a cave at its base. Follow the twists and turns of the stream bed.

By **1h25min** it looks as if a massive boulder blocks the way (❷) — perhaps it's the 'plug' that has come out of the mountainside above and ahead, leaving a cave? Follow waymarking (faded red and blue, newer green/red) to the right of the boulder, scrambling over a huge rockfall for five minutes. Then, to get back down to the stream bed, head towards the left-hand rock wall. CAIRNS will show you the way back to the stream bed, where you pick up the red waymarking again. Continue through a thicket of bushes. Waymarking will direct you around another rockfall, as you climb more steeply.

At **1h50min** a WATER TROUGH and a large oleander bush make a peaceful resting spot in amongst the rocks. Beyond here, look for waymarking on the left-hand side of the gorge, pointing uphill, away from the trough, and taking you into another scramble. Follow the waymarking carefully! Five minutes from the water trough the path flattens out, and the landscape opens up. A well-painted boulder (mostly red/green stripes) comes into sight on the left. Follow the arrow indicating 'LIVANIANA' — to the right. You skirt round a LARGE OLIVE TREE (❸; **2h**), as you climb up the right-hand side of the gorge. You will spot some faded blue waymarking as the path winds up the hillside through old terraced olive trees towards the rock face on your right.

Having hugged the rock face, the steep path rises to a LARGE WALLED ENCLOSURE WITH CHICKEN WIRE ON TOP (❹) directly in front of you. Turn left, keeping it close by on your right, and continue uphill through more terracing. Then turn right through a gap in the drystone wall. Continue to follow the waymarking. A few minutes after the gap in the wall, the path turns left, following a stone wall. A minute later there is a wonderful view down over the coast, and the CHURCH (❺) at **Livaniana** is just a few metres ahead of you. This is the upper part of the almost-

The old church at Aradhena, rising above the gorge

Bridge into Aradhena

deserted village of Livaniana, and you are at a junction (**2h45min**). *(The Shorter walk goes straight ahead here.)*

The main walk turns *sharply left*, avoiding the village: walk between the wall with chicken wire on the left and the wire fence on the right — you may notice a red waymark. The rocky path climbs along the right-hand side of a wall; keep beside the wall. When the walled and fenced enclosure ends, the waymarked path continues straight ahead. At this point you reach a rocky outcrop and, continuing along the ridge, you encounter another stone wall: keep this wall on your right and head across an open area; the sea is now in sight again. Ahead you can see the stone walls supporting your ongoing path as it climbs the hillside.

At **3h05min** the path opens out on a flatter area; look carefully for the waymarking here — and later, as you start to climb again in zigzags. Watch for the griffon vultures that are often seen here — it will help take your mind off the long haul — and they are likely to be breath-takingly close. A road is visible ahead cutting across the hillside; the path joins the ROAD (6) at just under the **3h30min**-mark, after a fairly steep climb. Turn left on this road and follow it in a bend to the right. There are magnificent views over Livaniana and the beaches below — you can see Lykkos, Finix and part of Loutro.

Follow the road over the hill and onto a plateau. Under 20 minutes from where the path met this road you round a bend and have a wonderful view of the White Mountains ... marred only by a concrete animal shed in the foreground. Pass this shed, ignoring a fork off to the right just before it.

Ten minutes later the road has turned away from the coast, behind the shed, and you are heading straight towards the mountains. Rock-strewn grazing land and animal enclosures lie off to the left.

The houses and old church of **Aradhena** come into sight (**4h15min**). When you arrive at a T-junction, turn left: you will see the IRON BRIDGE (7) that leads over the top of the gorge into Aradhena (the photos opposite and on page 123 were taken from this point). It is also highly likely that you will see griffon vultures here. Crossing the bridge is not for vertigo sufferers; although robust and safe enough for vehicles, it is made with quite large gaps between the slats, and if a car goes past the whole thing vibrates loudly!

The village, although mostly deserted, has signs of renovation. Until 1986 Aradhena was only approachable by the steep donkey paths visible down the sides of the gorge below. There is a small snack bar directly over the bridge, and the surroundings of the 14th-century church make a pleasant shaded place to sit. Or stay by the bridge to watch the bungee-jumpers...

To continue the walk, retrace your steps past the T-junction and keep straight ahead along the road. After three minutes (some 270m further on), just before a stone wall, head right on a track, passing under power cables. Then, after another 40m, look carefully on the left for a cairn, placed almost directly below the power cables, just before a wall on which there are red waymarks. Follow the wall, and fork left under an ancient olive tree. You are now on a rough old cobbled path (8).

Fifteen minutes from the T-junction the houses of Anopolis (still spelled with an 's' at the end, but pronounced Anopoli) come into view. At about this point the cobbles run out abruptly, but the waymarked path is clear as it heads downhill. Follow it between stone walls and turn left. Then, almost immediately (where the path meets a fence), walk left towards the houses of Anopolis. You come onto a road; follow this as it makes a tight bend to the right. Pass a small chapel on the left, surrounded by lovely shady holm oaks and, when you come to a T-junction, turn right on another road.

After 15 minutes, at a T-junction (where there is a taverna on the left), turn right to the village 'square' in **Anopolis** (**5h**). It is more of a circle, with a statue of Daskalogiannis in the middle. Head right and follow a sign for 'AG EIKATERINI'. Passing the last houses, the road goes on into a hairpin bend. There's a nice view looking back over the fertile plain around Anopolis.

Some 25 minutes from the square, when the road ends at a flat area, walk right towards a shrine. The path straight ahead here goes down to Loutro, 1h15min away. First, however, for an even more fantastic view and a very worthwhile detour, climb steeply up to the right from the shrine, to the church of **Agia Eikaterina** (9) with a fine viewing platform.

Then return to the path and descend *carefully* to Loutro; this path requires steady footwork. Ten minutes from the shrine ignore a path forking left, back to Anopolis. Some minutes later, join a bulldozed track. Head down to the right and after about 100m cairns on the left signal where you rejoin the path. When you next meet the track, more cairns point the way (straight over). The path crosses a gully.

Some 25 minutes later you come to a fork: the right fork goes to 'Finix'. Take the *left* fork, down to Loutro. Fifteen minutes later pass a SHRINE on the left (where Walk 25 begins) and head right, towards the village. Clamber through a stock control gate and in five minutes (**7h05min**) you're back in **Loutro** (O) — more than ready for a swim, as you have probably been out for more like 10 hours!

Walk 25: FROM LOUTRO TO HORA SFAKION

See map pages 120-121; see also photo on page 117
Distance: 7km/4.3mi; 2h
Grade: ●? moderate, with some scrambling (although there are no appreciable climbs/descents); you must be sure-footed and have a head for heights, especially after Sweetwater beach (danger of vertigo). E4-waymarked. *Very little shade*
Equipment: walking trainers, sunhat, picnic, water, swimwear
Picnic: Sweetwater beach (springs and some shade)
Access: bus to Hora Sfakion (Timetable 4); journey time about 2h. Then boat to Loutro: see Walk 23 page 104; voyage time 30min. Return by bus from Hora Sfakion (Timetable 4; as above)
Alternative walk: Tack this on to Walk 23 (7h05min) — or stay overnight in the area to explore Walks 22 and 24 as well.

Loutro is a wonderful, away-from-it-all backwater, perfect for really relaxing — particularly as there is no traffic, bar boats. From the ferry you will see the route heading east along the hillside above the coast.

Start the walk at **Loutro** HARBOUR (O): head up to the left of the Taverna Kri-kri, at the east end of the bay. The coastal path starts at an easily-visible SHRINE. (Walk 24 comes directly down the hillside in zigzags to this point.) Those who suffer from vertigo may experience difficulty in **15min**, as the path skirts the edge of the steep cliff, and again at the **30min**-point, where you cross a stretch of sandy scree.

Pass **Agios Stavros** chapel and descend to **Sweetwater Beach** (**1h**). Fresh springs gush from the mountainside here, and there are boats to and from Loutro and Hora Sfakion in high season. Continue over beach and rocks; **1h20min** from Loutro the path runs some 70m/200ft or more above the sea, and there is a sheer drop down to the right. This potentially vertiginous stretch — where you may meet goats coming the other way — lasts for 10-12 minutes.

When the path meets road, on a hairpin bend, turn right and walk into **Hora Sfakion** (O; **2h**). You reach the BUS STOP — and a host of other amenities — just as you come into the village.

Hora Sfakion from the sea. There are regular sailings to Loutro, Agia Roumeli, Sougia and Paleohora.

Walk 26: THE IMBROS GORGE • KOMITADES • HORA SFAKION

See also photos on pages 31 and opposite
Distance: 12km/7.4mi; 3h50min
Note: there is a small fee payable to enter the gorge.
Grade: ● fairly straightforward descent of 750m/2460ft in a gorge, but you must be sure-footed and agile
Equipment: walking trainers or boots, sunhat, picnic, water, swimming things
Picnic: in the shady gorge
Access: Hora Sfakion 🚌 to Imbros (Timetable 4); journey time about 1h45min. *Hint:* Sit on the left-hand side of the bus for the best views. Or 🚗 to Imbros; park near the entrance to the gorge (35° 15.233'N, 24° 10.286'E). Return by 🚌 from Hora Sfakion to Hania (Timetable 4); journey time 1h45min. 🚗 Motorists will find an 8-seater minibus by the taverna at the end of the gorge, to take you back to your car at Imbros.

Shorter walk: Imbros Gorge — Komitades (7km/4.3mi; 2h50min). ● Grade, equipment, access as main walk. Follow the main walk to Komitades and catch a Frangokastello–Hora Sfakion 🚌 there: buses depart about 14.15 and 16.50; *recheck at Hora Sfakion!* journey time 10min. Then 🚌 as above.

This is a really delightful amble through the now popular, pine tree-lined Imbros Gorge, which narrows and widens very dramatically in places — until you reach the south coast and the Libyan Sea. The bus rides are quite long, since you follow a winding route from the north to south coast and then back again, but these journeys enable you to see a good slice of Cretan countryside. It's a good walk for children, too.

Make it clear that you'll be walking the **Imbros Gorge**, and the bus will drop you at the start, by a TAVERNA in **Imbros** village (●). (There is another bus stop and parking area further south by another taverna at ⓐ: see map.) **Start out** by taking the lane beside the 'IMBROS GORGE' sign, and after 250m turn right on a track. This track becomes a footpath as it meets the stream bed.

At first the surroundings are not very gorge-like; soon after collecting your ticket you will be surrounded by Jerusalem sage, striking in spring and early summer. The route leads all the way to the coast; sometimes the path is in the gorge, sometimes it runs beside it to avoid large boulders. Once you are on the route, it's virtually impossible to lose your way. Anywhere around here is a good place to picnic. By **50min** into the walk, you will be briefly on a donkey trail, the old main donkey trail to Sfakia, still beautifully cobbled.

Just past the NARROWEST PART OF THE GORGE (❶; where you can touch the walks on both sides), there's a small REST AREA; in summer, you may find enterprising people here selling raki and ouzo, well as cooling drinks.

At **2h20min** you can see the south coast and the sea ahead in the middle distance. You should just be able to make out the 14th-century Venetian fort, Frangokastello (shown on page 33). By **2h30min** or sooner, you will come to a second ticket kiosk at the exit from the

Different aspects of the Imbros Gorge: at first the setting is not very gorge-like, and you are surrounded by Jerusalem sage.

gorge (❷). There's another small REST AREA here as well. Five minutes later, ignore a track up to the left; continue along the E4 in the stony streambed, to emerge on the main road by a chapel on the right. Turn right, passing a taverna on the left, and walk on to the village ahead, **Komitades** (**2h50min**). Either wait here for a bus *(Shorter walk)* or walk on to Hora Sfakion, an hour away.

To continue to Hora Sfakion, keep on the road and, 10 minutes later (where you join the main Hora Sfakion road at a T-junction; ❸), turn left. You can wait for the Hania bus here but, if it is full, it may not stop. By **3h50min** you're in the centre of **Hora Sfakion** (❹), its small harbour bristling with *cafeneions* and tavernas.

Walk 27: KARES (ASKYFOU) • ASFENDOS • AGIOS NEKTARIOS

Distance: 14.2km/8.8mi; 5h10min
Grade: ● moderate but long, with an ascent of about 220m/720ft and descent of 950m/3100ft, the latter part in a gorge
Equipment: walking trainers, sunhat, picnic, water
Picnic: in a shady spot on the plain or round Goni
Access: Hora Sfakion 🚌 to 'Sfakian Bakery' junction in Askyfou (Timetable 4); journey time about 1h20min. (See main text for more detail about this bus stop.) Return by 🚌 from Agios Nektarios to Hora Sfakion (not in the timetables, but departs between 15.30-16.00 daily); journey time 20 minutes. Alternatively, pre-arrange a Sfakia taxi or call a taxi when you are nearing Ag Nektarios (tel: 69726 90139). Then 🚌 to Hania (Timetable 4); journey time about 2h

One of our favourite walks, this excursion combines a good bus ride, covering masses of ground, with a walk across the lovely plain shown overleaf and then over some easy mountain terrain. We finish with a descent through a gorge, with the Libyan Sea as our goal. The road that the bus follows is the route along which thousands of war-weary soldiers trudged in 1941, when they withdrew, under relentless air attack, to the south coast. The walk leads you through a gorgeous chunk of Cretan countryside — spectacular anytime, but particularly picturesque in spring, when the plain at Askyfou is dotted with poppies and the gorge is lined with bright yellow Jerusalem sage.

Be ready to get off the bus when, having wound up and round hillsides, you see the Askyfou plain come into sight below left. Before you leave the bus, it passes an eye-catching old Turkish fort, strategically sited on a hillock mid-plain. Then the bus passes a first turn-off left to Kares; you want the *next* turn-off left for 'KARES', opposite the isolated 'Sfakian Bakery' on the main road (and just before the large domed church).

Start the walk from the BAKERY JUNCTION (⓪) in **Askyfou**: head south down into the hamlet of **Kares**, walking towards the plain and *forking right immediately,* following signs for the War Museum. Pass the MUSEUM (❶) on your right and head out of the village. Take the next left turning, a surfaced track. This track will take you across the plain itself via fields of vegetables planted and tended by the Askyfou villagers. Within a few minutes, ignore a turn to the left, then pass a WELL on the left. Soon, at a cross-tracks, turn left, passing another old WELL. Some 15 minutes from Kares (**20min**) the track becomes asphalted as it meets a road. Join the road, keeping straight ahead.

The road rises as you approach **Goni**, the next village, and then curves round to the right, skirting the village. It ends by an old building with 'No. 20' painted on it (❷). There is a WALK INFORMATION BOARD here, and GREEN/WHITE WAYMARKING begins. Take the track straight ahead (initially surfaced), to the right of the building. It bends

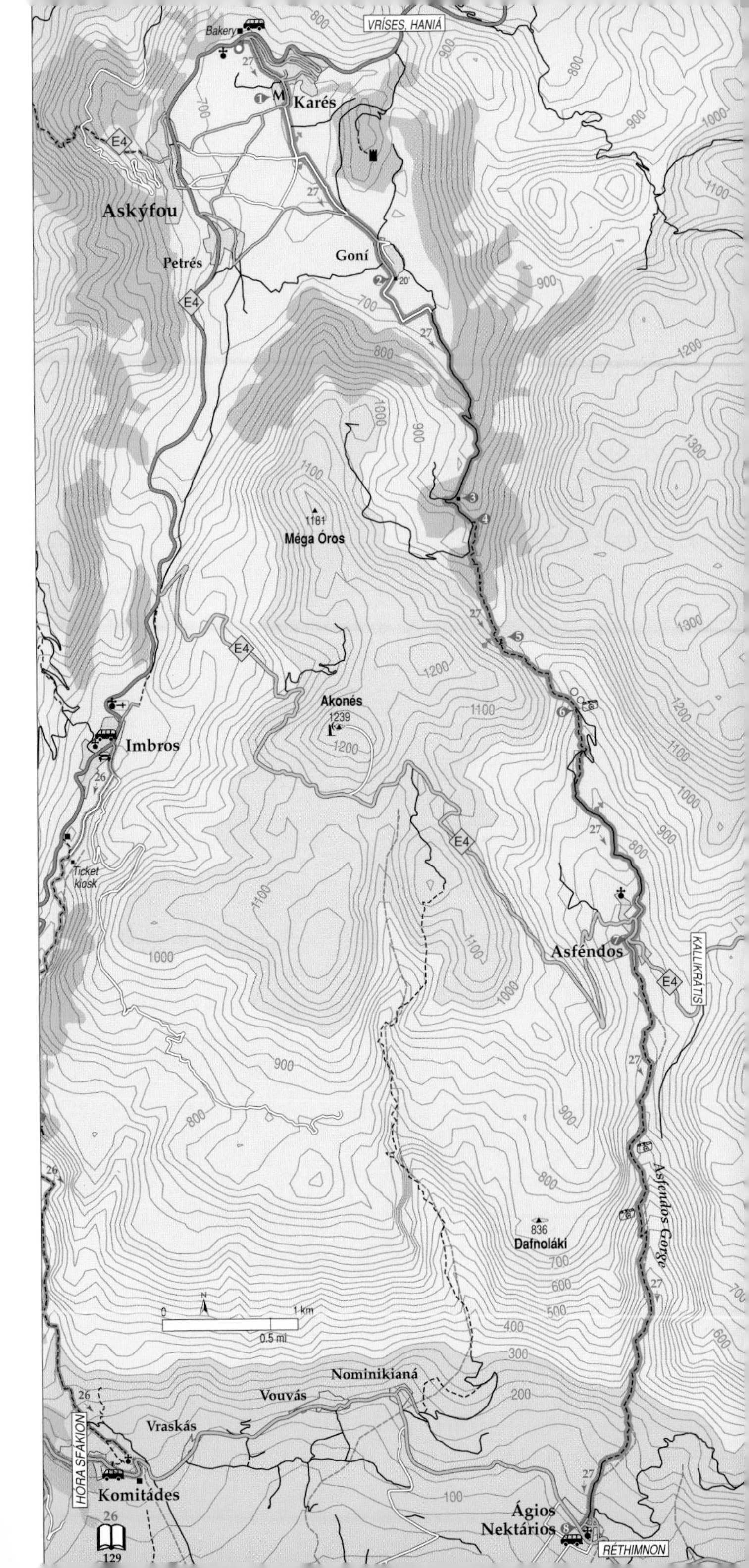

VRÍSES, HANIÁ
Bakery
Karés
Askýfou
Petrés
Goní
E4
Méga Óros
1181
Akonés
1239
Imbros
Ticket kiosk
Asféndos
KALLIKRÁTIS
Asféndos Gorge
Dafnoláki
836
Nominikianá
Vouvás
Vraskás
HÓRA SFAKION
Komitádes
Ágios Nektários
RÉTHIMNON
0
1 km
0.5 mi
129

round and away from Goni. Follow the track straight on, ignoring grassy tracks off. Some 30 minutes from Kares, Goni will be directly behind you, as you head south into the valley.

Ten minutes beyond Goni, keep right at a fork. Pass through any mesh gates; the route starts to rise. At **1h10min**, just past a SHEPHERD'S DWELLING (❸) on the left, where the track divides, turn left and curl back on yourself. As you walk up this track, look for a path running below you on the left. You need to find a way down onto this wide path, then follow it for 250m, heading due south towards the 'V' ahead. Then look for a smaller path going off left at a CAIRN and a RED ARROW

The White Mountains (Levka Ori) from the Askyfou plain

(❹; **1h30min**). The waymarked path climbs to an open grassy area, then levels out. Ahead on the hillside you will notice some stone walls that underpin the ongoing path. Aiming for those walls, follow the path past a WATER TROUGH and under two large kermes oaks. The way leads up and continues to the left on the stone-built section ahead. The footpath widens out on the walls, which zigzag up to the PASS (❺; **1h45min**).

From here a well-established path gradually starts the descent to the sea. The route descends across another open grassy area, past an ANIMAL SHELTER and a group of trees set off to the left. Reaching the far side of the flat grazing land, you will catch sight of the distant sea for the first time. A STONY TRACK (❻) leads off from here, 30m/yds from the grassy area. Take the path which goes off to the right of the track. It descends, meeting the track again after 10 minutes. Cross the track and look for the rather indistinct path again. (It's worth taking the path as it is more direct and cuts some loops off the track.)

At **2h40min** pass a WATER DEPOSIT on the left, and stay on the track. Be aware that you are heading for the V of the gorge ahead. When you meet an asphalt road on a bend, walk straight ahead; the very basic houses of **Asfendos** come into sight (**2h50min**). The village CHURCH is high up on the right. A few minutes later you come to a wire mesh animal gate; go through and turn left on the road to Kallikratis. At the next junction, a Y-fork 170m further on, go right (❼). (There may be small signs here — left to Rethimnon and Kallikratis, right to Hania and Hora Sfakion.)

In three minutes the asphalt stops; continue on a path, past some old houses and on into the countryside again. The V becomes a U in the distance, the left-hand side of it opening outwards as you near the gorge. The path is thickly edged with Jerusalem sage — a glorious bright yellow mass in spring. About half an hour from Asfendos there are clear signs that part of this very old path was formerly paved. You can see the gorge now, ahead of you. Forty minutes from Asfendos (**3h20min**), you will see the sea in the cleft ahead, and scree comes in on the right. Five minutes further on, pass a waymarked boulder. The path then does a double bend and zigzags down the hillside. Although you are high, the gorge is too layered to pose any problems for vertigo sufferers.

Keep on zigzagging down the hillside amongst any goats and sheep that might be about. About 1h30min from Asfendos (**4h10min**) you will be able to see the beach and sea below and ahead of you. If you come to any forks in the path, just continue in the same direction, down the side of the gorge. Before long, you will find that the route criss-crosses the dry river bed. Ten minutes from the start of these river bed crossings, you will be high above the dry river bed again.

Some 2h20min from Asfendos (**5h**) the path divides; go left. After a few minutes a fence comes in from the right. The path comes down to a gravelly area, where there is a CONCRETE BUILDING on the left. Walk past the building and then between the few houses of **Agios Nektarios**, to the south coast road. A CHURCH lies to the left (❽; **5h10min**). Turn right on the main road to head for Hora Sfakion, or meet a pre-arranged taxi here. A bus for Hora Sfakion will pass at about 16.00.

Walk 28: CIRCUIT VIA MONI PREVELI

See also photos on pages 12-13 and 35 (bottom)
Distance: 11.3km/7mi; 3h30min
Grade: ● easy-moderate, with descents/ascents of about 350m/ 1150ft; ***but you must be sure-footed and agile on the path above the river and for the descent to Palm Beach.***
Equipment: walking trainers, sunhat, picnic, water, swimming things, suitable dress for Moni Preveli (trousers for men, longish skirts for women)
Picnic: by the bridge at the start
Access: 🚗 to/from the arched bridge 3.5km southeast of Asomatos on the road to Moni Preveli (Car tour 6; 35° 10.441'N, 24° 27.958'E); there is plenty of parking — either by the roadside or over the new concrete bridge, by the side of the duck pond.

Alternative walks

1 To Palm Beach and return (10km/ 6mi; 2h30min). ● Grade as main walk (descent/ascent of about 300m/ 1000ft); equipment and access as main walk. Follow the main walk to the CAR PARK (③). Leave it via the gate in the eastern fence (the pay booth is at the western side). Follow the path on the western side of the river, with the gorge below on your right and the asphalt road to the monastery on your left and above you. This path (later a track) goes back to the bridge at ⓞ.

2 Circuit from Asomatos, for those travelling by bus (18km/11.2mi; 5h15min). ● Grade as main walk, but considerably longer and with descents/ascents of about 450m/ 1475ft overall; equipment as main walk. Access: Plakias 🚌 from Rethimnon to/from Asomatos (Timetable 15); the return bus leaves Asomatos a few minutes after departure from Plakias; journey time 35min. The bus drops you off in the centre of Asomatos by the junction to Plakias and Moni Preveli; follow the signposted road, turning left after 1.5km (ⓐ). After another 2km you come to the bridge where the main walk starts; pick up the notes below and return the same way.
NB: *In summer only, you can catch a bus from Moni Preveli back to Rethimnon (Timetable 14); journey time 45min — thus halving the distance and saving the long ascent.*

This is a beautiful circuit, although rather long if you travel by bus. If you don't mind hitch-hiking or taking an extra bus, it can be cut short at various points should the heat prove too exhausting or the temptations of flopping on the beach too much. The views down into the gorge on Alternative walk 1 are just spectacular!

Moni Preveli

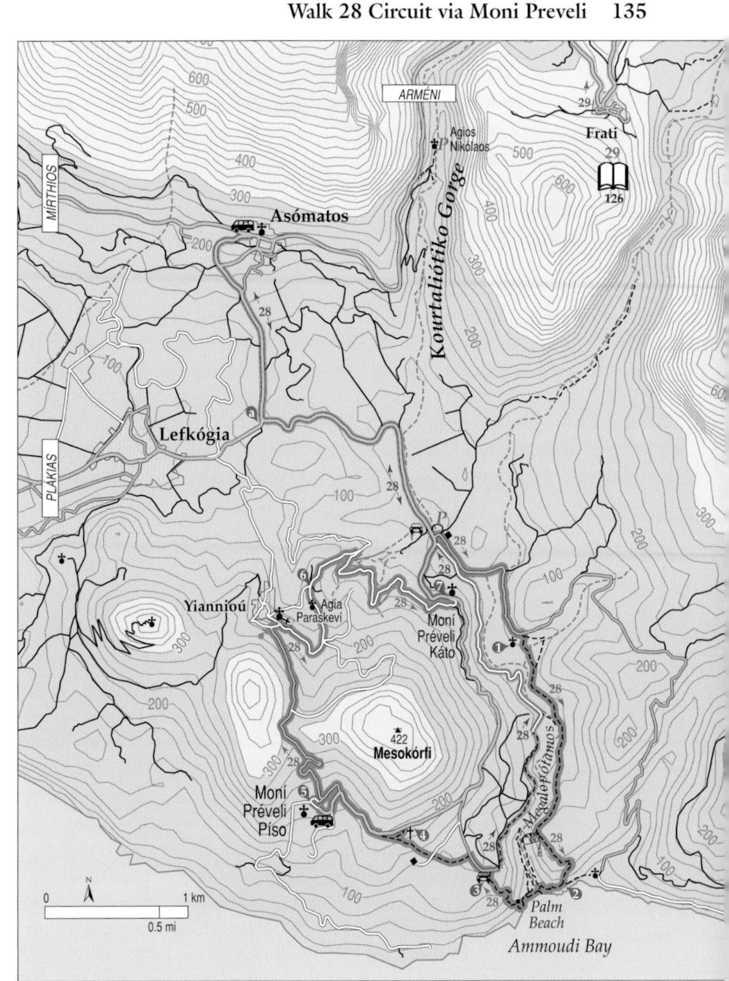

The walk starts at the STEEPLY ARCHED BRIDGE (◎) shown on pages 12-13, on the road to Moni Preveli and Palm Beach. Walk in front of the Taverna Gefyra (Gefyra means 'bridge' in Greek), following the road along the east side of the **Megalopotamos** — one of the few rivers in Crete that flows all year round — a lovely picnic setting. You cross another COBBLED BRIDGE in 10 minutes, and follow the road round to the right. About five minutes or so later (after 45m), you pass a gated and locked turning right to a DERELICT MONASTERY (❶). A few metres further on, turn right and right again (beside a fence blocking off a parade of beehives ahead), dipping down into a gully. Follow the narrow path round the left side of the gully and cross a small watercourse. The path then continues on the other side of the gully, somewhat precipitous in places.

The path circles clockwise round this valley, well defined, with CAIRNS and occasional RED WAYMARKS. As you make for the saddle ahead, you go through a stock control gate and then the path opens out to give you views back towards Asomatos. But a tall wire fence prevents you from getting close to the edge and looking down into the gorge. This fence continues, just to the right of your path. Soon you pass under some electricity cables (**50min**). Just afterwards, near a small TRANSMITTER to your right, the Libyan Sea and Palm Beach at Preveli come into full view, looking *unbelievably* inviting.

Still with the fence on your right, follow the well-trodden path as it turns left. Where the fence bends sharply left and appears to block your path, the path will lead you to a opening — or there may be a gate to negotiate. From here turn right (RED DOT WAYMARKS). Keep the fence on your right and take the well-worn path that appears to just drop over the edge of the steep terrain. Zigzag down this path, which demands agility and sure-footedness. As you descend you will see a large taverna (with road access) on the neighbouring beach. Keep descending, taking whichever route seems easiest, all the while keeping the fence to your right. You are heading for a PATH THAT LINKS THE TWO BEACHES (❷).

When you reach it, turn right and five minutes later you arrive at **Palm Beach** (**1h15min**). After a swim and a rest, wade across the river to the far side of the beach (where there's a café/bar in summer) and climb the rocks at the water's edge here, rounding the headland. Then take the steps up to the top of the cliff.

Within about 20 minutes you emerge at a PARKING AREA (❸). Leave it via the vehicle entrance. After about three minutes a BLUE SIGN on your left directs you through a gate towards Moni Preveli. You pass a building on your right, and from here a track between fences funnels you in the right direction. Go straight over a junction (another BLUE SIGN) and head up a slope towards the main road. Where you join the road, take a few minutes to hop over the fence and look at the MEMORIAL TO PEACE AND REMEMBRANCE (❹).

Turn left on the road and in a couple of minutes you round a bend and the monastery is now in view, 10 minutes away. You can fill up with water at **Moni Preveli** (❺; **2h**) and have a wander round, if you have the proper clothing with you. In *summer only,* you can catch a bus back to Rethimnon here; it travels via Asomatos.

To continue, leave the monastery and walk back along the asphalt road to the first right-hand bend, here take the road off to the left (or take the short cut shown on the map. This road winds its way up the hill to a SADDLE (**2h20min**) and down the other side. In another quarter of an hour you are just outside **Yianniou**. Take a sharp right on another track that goes downhill about 70m/yds before a FOUNTAIN/ WATERING HOLE on your left (just before entering the village). Almost immediately you come to a T-junction by a white-washed church: turn right. Soon the track bends left and rises steeply.

At the crest of this hill, the track splits three ways. Turn left and pass the church of **Agia Paraskevi**, on a ridge. Some 150m past this church, keep half-right downhill on the main track (❻). Five minutes later (after 400m), turn right and follow a gently-rippling irrigation channel down to the asphalt road at the derelict monastery of **Kato Preveli** (❼; 'lower Preveli'). This original

'Moni Preveli', shown on page 35, was abandoned at the time of the Ottoman conquest.

Turn left and continue on the asphalt road for 10 minutes, until you reach the STEEPLY ARCHED BRIDGE you crossed at the start of your walk (**◎; 3h30min**). Pick up your transport here or, if you came by bus, stay on the asphalt road for an hour, to return to Asomatos (remember to turn right at the next T-junction; ⓐ).

Palm (Preveli) Beach, the palm-fringed oasis where the Megalopotamos empties into the crystal-clear waters of the Libyan Sea.

Walk 29: ANO MEROS • TRIPITI • ANO MEROS

Distance: 9km/5.6mi; 4h
Grade: ●❢ fairly strenuous ascent and descent of 600m/1970ft. The final ascent is not waymarked and involves some clambering; you must be sure-footed and have a head for heights. *Little shade en route*
Equipment: walking trainers, long socks/trousers in spring, sunhat, windproof, picnic, water
Picnic: Kaloidena chapel
Access: 🚗 to/from Ano Meros: park in the main street, near the church (35° 11.237'N, 24° 39.659'E).
Short walk: Kaloidena chapel (2.4km/1.5mi; 40min). ● Easy, with an ascent/descent of only 160m/500ft. A pleasant leg-stretcher during a car tour, this gives you a bit of exercise and leads to a pretty picnic spot with a spring and fine views. Follow the main walk for the first 20 minutes; return the same way.

Kedros is the elongated mountain on the western side of the Amari Valley, rising to 1775m/5822ft. This walk takes you up its flanks to a viewpoint on a lesser peak, Tripiti, from where you will enjoy a tremendous outlook. (If you are driving, watch for 12th-century frescoed Moni Agios Ioannis Theologos — on the left between Gerakari and Ano Meros. Gerakari, by the way, was levelled by the Germans during World War II in retaliation for the abduction of General Kreipe — a story detailed in the books by Moss and Leigh Fermor on page 6.)

Start out by leaving the CHURCH (**O**) of **Ano Meros** on your right: head southeast on the main road, towards Hordaki. Immediately you enjoy a fantastic outlook towards Psiloritis. Ignore the first small,

stepped turning (by the telephone box) off to the right. Take the *next* right turn — well-paved steps (which *may* be signposted to Tripiti, Kaloidena or Gerakari). At the top of the flight of steps turn left; then, almost immediately, go right.

The concrete track rises steeply; when it ends, ignore the turning to the right and take the path on the left, heading uphill. Keep a wire fence close by on the right, and turn left when you come to a crossing wire fence. Walk over some small boulders and around the end of another wire fence, to come to a gravel track opposite a large WATER TANK (➊; **8min**).

Turn right on the track. Two minutes later stay on the main track, leaving another track off to the left. Head towards the mountains; there is a valley down to the right. In places you will see vestiges of old water-channelling down the middle of the track.

At **20min** fork off right to see the restored chapel of **Kaloidena** (➋) — part of a monastery destroyed by the Turks in 1821. The chapel, with its splendid view, is above a gated shady concrete picnic area, where a clear spring gushes by the gate. Looking out over the Amari Valley you can still see part of the Platys River.

To continue the walk, head back to the fork in the track and head up to the right. At the next T-junction go left on an asphalt road, leaving an old farm building up to your right. There are the remains of an old WATERMILL down to the left just past the junction. After 200m you go through a GATEWAY and pass a track off to the left; turn sharp right immediately, on a weak track (there may be a waymark on the rock ahead). After a little over 50m, when the track peters out, take a path going up to the left (trousers or long socks will come in handy now).

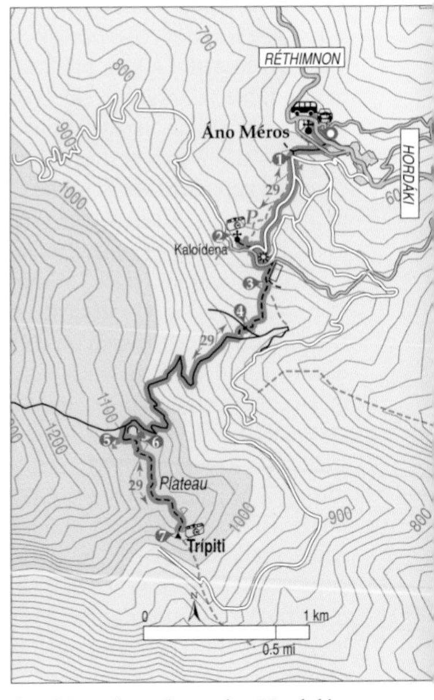

Ano Meros from the road to Hordaki

On the ascent and descent from Tripiti, your views encompass Mount Samitos and a reservoir in the Ligiotis Valley.

Beyond a STOCK CONTROL GATE the path turns left at the end of a WALLED VINEYARD. As the fencing curves round the end of the vineyard, the path forks: go right (❸). Look left for a large CAIRN here, by some kermes oaks.

Very shortly cross over a DRIED-UP WATERCOURSE with collapsed sides. The route is very sparsely waymarked with CAIRNS, but keep it in mind that you want to climb onto and over the ridge ahead. At this point it's also worth noting a square-cornered gap ahead, high in the mountainside — that's where you're going!

When you join a track (**50min**), *take note of the spot* (❹) so that you can pick up the path again on your return. Turn left on the track and make your way through a GATE. (If you meet a fence before the track, walk right to find the track, then go through the gate.) There is a CAIRN on the far side of the track opposite where you came up to it, indicating your ongoing path. When you next meet track (**1h**) turn right and keep heading uphill. There *are* paths short-cutting loops off this track, but you may find yourselves following goat-paths to nowhere; on the ascent it is easier to keep to the track. Use the short-cuts to descend, when you can see where you are heading. Soon the 'square-cornered' gap in the ridge ahead can be clearly seen.

In **1h50min** you reach the TOP OF THE RIDGE. Up to the left is a smelly CAVE/STOCKADE! The track soon ends at a grey WATER STORAGE TANK (❺) on the right. If a mist has descended it is *not* advisable to climb beyond this point because there is no waymarking. Hopefully conditions will allow you to press on to a more inviting goal.

When you are abreast of the storage tank, turn left uphill and walk to the right of the stone outcrop in front of you, towards a LONE KERMES OAK (❻). Walk to the right of that tree with its holly-like leaves, and down across a small PLATEAU/GRAZING AREA (there are some large cairns). From here you can see a small concrete trig point marking the Tripiti viewpoint. Make your own way, scrambling up to it where you feel is easiest. Approaching from the left is probably best. There is a cairn at the top on the left, and the **Tripiti** TRIG POINT is to the right (❼; **2h10min**). This is a tremendous viewpoint; it feels miles from anywhere. You look out over the Mesara Plain — where Festos and Agia Triada are sited — and across to the little island of Paximadia, just off the coast. The peninsula that juts out into the sea from Agia Galini is also visible in the distance.

Retrace your steps from here, taking advantage of some of the short-cut paths. You should be back at the CHURCH (⓿) in **Ano Meros** in **4h**.

Walk 30: CIRCUIT FROM MIXOROUMA VIA FRATI

See also photo on page 37
Distance: 13.4km/8.3mi; 3h55min
Grade: ● moderate; straightforward ascents/descents of about 400m/1300ft overall, on good shepherds' 4X4 tracks. The ascent is divided into two main sections, one at the start, the second about halfway through the walk.

Equipment: walking trainers or boots, sunhat, picnic, water
Picnic: Megalopotamos River
Access: 🚌 to/from Rethimnon (Timetable 1); journey time 1h. Then 🚌 to/from Mixorouma (Timetable 20); journey time about 45min. Or 🚗 to/from Mixorouma: park on the main road near the bus stop (35° 13.131'N, 24° 30.437'E).

This is a lovely walk in a well cultivated valley with spectacular views of the high hills and crags around the Kourtaliotiko Gorge. In spring, there are wildflowers galore. Some frescoed Byzantine churches lie along your route, and there is the opportunity to stop almost exactly halfway round — for a picnic at the Megalopotamos and again at the village of Frati, where there is a *cafeneion*.

The bus stops in the village of **Mixorouma** along the main road heading south to Spili. **To start the walk** (**O**), continue walking east towards Spili, until you reach a sign denoting the eastern end of the village. Just alongside the last building in the village turn right on an asphalt road signposted to the village of 'MOURNE'. As the road heads steeply downhill towards the river, ignore any right or left turns for the moment. After you cross the river on a BRIDGE (**5min**), your road begins to climb. Look out for the RUINED MILL on the left set among citrus trees. Continue on the road, climbing quite steeply, with several sharp bends.

About 10 minutes after the bridge (**15min**), you will have rounded a left-hand bend and will see a small farm building ahead on the left. Just before you reach this building, take a CONCRETE TRACK (**1**) heading right, uphill (it soon becomes a dirt and stone track). Ignore any minor tracks left and right and just head uphill on what is obviously the main track. You will pass through two STOCK CONTROL GATES, the second just by a house near the top of the hill; please leave them as you find them.

Before long you rejoin the asphalt road (**25min**). Turn right into the village of **Mourne**. At the Y-FORK (**2**; **30min**) with the trig point on a crag above and ahead of you, take the wider road round to the left and go left at another junction almost immediately. About four minutes later (200m), turn right at the T-junction. Turn right again at the next junction 70m further on. Make a third right turn after another 75m, heading uphill and out of the village. (Some 30m/yds to your left at this point is a spring/washing area signposted 'TRADITIONAL FOUNT'). Then you come to the CEMETERY church of **Agios Georgios** (**3**; **45min**), which has some stunning 14th-century frescoes inside.

Leaving Agios Georgios, turn right and continue steeply uphill on a minor road. Follow this towards the top of the ridge. Ten minutes after leaving the church, turn right on a wider road (**55min**). After a short time, the views open out. After

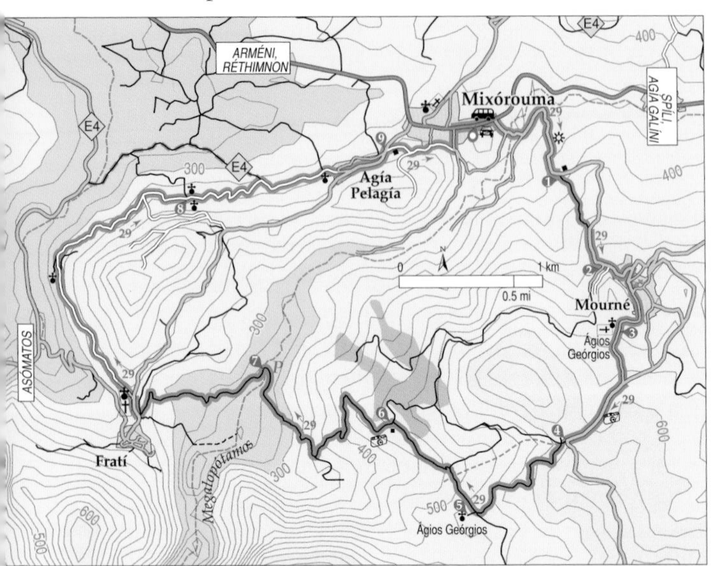

600m, at the highest point on this road, you reach a crossroads with a sign pointing left 'TO COAST' (4); *ignore* this and continue ahead. But just 30m further on, what has now become a dirt track splits three ways: take the track on the left (**1h10min**). Follow this for 15 minutes, to a crossroads (**1h25min**). You will continue downhill to the right, but

first walk forward 60m to explore the next church — another **Agios Georgios** (5) with more frescoes.

Returning to the start of your diversion, continue down the dirt track, ignoring minor turns left and right. After crossing a small WATERCOURSE (**1h35min**), turn left. Ignore a couple of tracks going off left, and your track will begin to climb again. Ten minutes after the watercourse turn left at the T-JUNCTION (4; **1h45min**) by a small building with corrugated roof. The views to Frati and the Kourtaliotiko Gorge become quite spectacular along this section. Continue down the dirt track, which zigzags and becomes very steep. Shortly after one left-hand bend heavily reinforced with concrete and with rain gullies, the main track swings right and flattens out. At this point, ignore the track heading left downhill into the heart of a large olive grove.

Soon you reach the bottom of the valley at a CONCRETE BRIDGE over the river **Megalopotamos** (7; **2h**) — a pleasant picnic spot. From here the track winds uphill for about 25 minutes, into the village of **Frati** (**2h25min**), where you could take a break at the taverna or *cafeneion*.

Turn right on the asphalt road past some rental apartments. When you reach the CEMETERY CHURCH two minutes later, turn left on a minor road. This road soon becomes a dirt track and contours around a hillside high above the road leading into the Kourtaliotiko Gorge. Continue along this track, ignoring all side turnings. Eventually you will pass between TWO CHURCHES (8; **3h10min**), in an olive grove. Some 20 minutes later, the E4 SIGN joins from the left, and there is a waymarking sign on an olive tree on your left (**3h30min**). Keep ahead. Five minutes later, pass another CHURCH on your right; head right, uphill, here. The track becomes concrete and then asphalt as you enter the village of **Agia Pelagia**.

As the road from Frati joins yours from the right, continue ahead through the village. About 20m/yds past the last house, take the concrete track heading right and slightly uphill by the E4 MARKER POLE (9; **3h45min**). Pass a FARM BUILDING on your right (with a wind pump on the roof), and bear left when you meet another track. The village of Mixorouma is now visible to your left. At the end of the track, there is a wide open space with a spring ahead of you. Take the road heading 90° left, which meets the main road through **Mixorouma** in the centre of the village. Turn right to the BUS STOP (O; **3h55min**).

View to Frati

Walk 31: THE KAMARES CAVE

Distance: 10km/6.2mi; 6h
Grade: ● a very strenuous climb and descent of 1100m/3600ft; you must be sure-footed and agile. E4 waymarking poles interspersed with cairns; plenty of water en route
Equipment: walking trainers or boots, sunhat, torch, picnic, water container, walking pole/s

Picnic: anywhere en route; there is ample shade
Access: 🚗 to/from Kamares; leave your car down off the main road, outside the church (35° 9.170'N, 24° 49.197'E). There is also a 🚌 from Rethimnon on Mondays-Fridays (Timetable 19), but timings are too tight to complete the walk.

This is somewhat of an aerobic exercise to a huge cave where the original cache of elaborate Minoan pottery known as Kamares Ware was found; it is now on display in the museum in Iraklion. The splendid cave, with a mouth 42m wide and 19m high (135ft x 62ft), is large and explorable. If you go to the back, and left of centre, search carefully and you will find the opening down on the floor, about 5m/15ft wide, where the pottery was found, in a fissure. For experienced climbers and walkers with the appropriate gear, Kamares is a good starting/finishing point for expeditions to the Nidha Plateau and Psiloritis.

Start out from the CHURCH in **Kamares** (⭘). Head east through the village. There's one of several pleasant old *cafeneions* just along on the left from the church. At the first fork, where there is a telegraph pole in the middle, keep straight on uphill (ignore Odos Ay Georgiou going off to the right). Within a few moments, at a three-way junction, fork left up 25TH MARCH STREET.

At the top of the hill you meet the main road. Cross straight over, onto an old concreted road. There are 'KAMARES' signs and maps on the wall at the left — and there may well still be a handwritten sign in German saying 'Only on Foot' ('Nur zu Fuss') — a nice bit of understatement. After a five-minute pull uphill the concrete ends, and rough track continues. Look up to the right and notice the first E4 signpost. The path starts just beyond it, turning hard back off the track; be sure to turn right here (*don't* go ahead towards the water tank). Remember to re-secure any stock control gates. The path turns steeply uphill, and the next E4 mark is on a tree. Keep your eye out for CAIRNS in the absence of E4 waymarking. Soon after the tree the path turns left and a WATER PIPE IN A CONCRETE CHANNEL (❶) starts on the right. This conduit accompanies you most of the way uphill, and several water troughs provide cold drinking water.

The path meets a track at a T-junction (**15min**; stock control gate); walk to the left and pick up the path again going up to the right, at the end of some ANIMAL DRINKING WELLS. The path turns right and forks (❷) just after an E4 waymark; crossing the hillside, look for CAIRNS to be sure of the route. As the path approaches the edge of a ravine, you have a fantastic view. From the viewpoint head back the way you've come and in three minutes you will be at a TROUGH where fresh water pours in off the mountainside.

In **1h30min**, as you climb into a band of trees, more CAIRN WAYMARKING starts. Ten minutes later, look left for a place to cut through the trees — mostly cypress

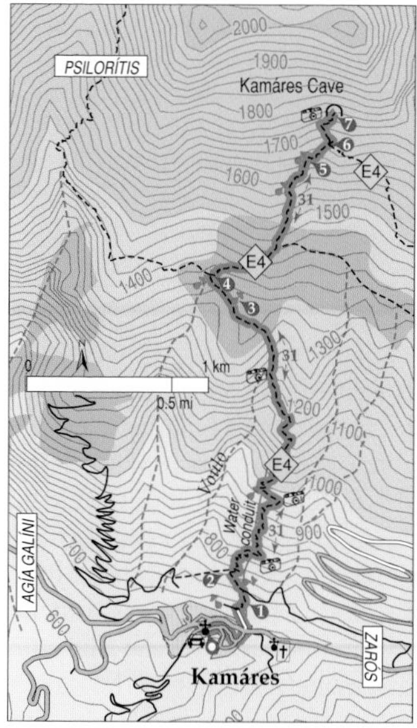

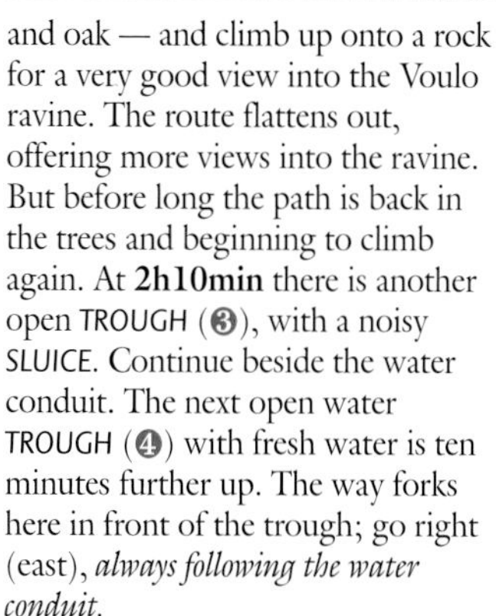

and oak — and climb up onto a rock for a very good view into the Voulo ravine. The route flattens out, offering more views into the ravine. But before long the path is back in the trees and beginning to climb again. At **2h10min** there is another open TROUGH (❸), with a noisy SLUICE. Continue beside the water conduit. The next open water TROUGH (❹) with fresh water is ten minutes further up. The way forks here in front of the trough; go right (east), *always following the water conduit.*

Now the way is very steep and rough; you need to be sure-footed. Having swung round from the east and continued uphill — still guided by E4 signs — you will come to another WATER TROUGH. Five minutes later, having struggled up to a CONCRETE CISTERN (❺), the path continues up to the right — across the front of the cistern. Fifteen minutes later the waymarks take you scrambling almost vertically up rocks. Five minutes later you will see the lip of the cave above, to the right of the path. At a BOULDER MARKED WITH FADED RED ARROWS, the path forks (❻; **3h**). Head left, towards two lone kermes oaks. In **3h30min** you will be at the top, in the mouth of the **Kamares Cave** (❼) — a pleasant place to relax before exploring.

Then retrace your steps to **Kamares** village (**O**; **6h**).

At the mouth of the enormous cave

Walk 32: ELEFTHERNA

Distance: 7km/4.3mi; 1h45min (or up to 4h with diversions)
Grade: ● fairly easy ups and downs of about 150m/500ft, but some steep steps; a short part of the route is E4 waymarked
Equipment: walking trainers, sunhat, picnic, water, *torch*

Picnic: Byzantine tower or the Hellenistic bridge (1h-point)
Access: 🚌 to/from Rethimnon (Timetable 1); journey time 1h. Then 🚌 to/from Archaia Eleftherna (Timetable 18); journey 1h. Or 🚗: park in the centre (35° 19.416'N, 24° 40.590'E).

This is a short walk in a lush green valley of olive, orange, cypress and pine trees — ablaze with wild flowers and cyclamen in spring. The spectacularly-sited Dorian city-state of Eleftherna (10th century BC) and a gem of a Hellenistic bridge are the main attractions. With the opening of a new museum and the necropolis in June 2016 (after an archaeological dig lasting some 30 years) there is far more to see than ever before. Unfortunately we went to press before we could recheck how much the site has changed in the last couple of years, but no doubt there will be many improvements. Do visit the museum either before or after your walk to make the most of the day.

Start out in the centre of **Archaia Eleftherna** (**O**): follow the road signed to the 'ACROPOLIS – CISTERNS' for 350m to the TAVERNA, where an INTERPRETATION BOARD in the car park shows you where you plan to walk and tells you about the ancient sites. Take the path immediately to the right of the taverna. In a minute you come to the BYZANTINE TOWER (**1**) shown opposite; it rises on a north-pointing ridge between two streams, with steep drops on either side — an ideal defensive position for the ancient acropolis. This walk will take you to the bottom of the western valley (on your left as you face the tower), then north beyond where the two valleys meet, and back up the spine of the ridge.

Follow the ancient cobblestone path to the left of the tower and then go straight ahead for a few minutes, before making a sharp left turn downhill (**2**). (To the right, the smaller path continuing to the north is the one you'll be returning on at the end of the walk.) Immediately on your left, as you round the bend, you'll see a row of ancient ROCK-CUT CISTERNS supported by massive stone columns; they are thought to be Roman or pre-Roman.

The path continues downhill, passing a limestone cliff on the left and a (dry) spring with water troughs. A minute later you come to a T-junction, where a track goes off to the left. Here take the earthen trail to the right; it curves left and, in one minute, you reach another T-JUNCTION (**3**). Go right (north) on the path with the black/yellow (E4) waymark. About three to four minutes along this path (250m), turn left down some earthen steps to an E4 MARKER POLE. At the E4 pole, turn left on the path with the rustic handrail that cuts through an olive grove. At the end of this path, cross the stream bed and turn right immediately, to follow the stream (E4 MARKER on a tree). About 30m further on, head half-left on steps leading up the bank. You emerge on a narrow fenced-in path, with an olive grove on your left and pines on your right. At the end of this short path, next to an E4 MARKER POLE, turn half-left up the next set of steps. When you meet a road (❹; **30min**), *don't* follow the E4 waymarks up the steps; turn right on the road. In a few minutes, at the first hairpin bend to the right, you can see the new MUSEUM and ancient NECROPOLIS (❺) across the valley (it's just 15 minutes there and back, but you may end up spending the day…).

From the bend, head north on a track. This track hairpins twice as it descends to the stream bed, eventually crossing it over a small concrete WATER DUCT (a small wall on the right). About 25 paces on from here, look out for an ANCIENT STEPPED PATH (❻) climbing off to the right — your return route up the central ridge. For the moment, stay ahead on the track which crosses ANOTHER CONCRETE DUCT, gradually rising. When the track bends sharp right, take the path dipping down to the left at the apex of this first bend (open and re-close the wire fence).

This steep and narrow path clings to a ledge on the eastern side of the valley, before descending to the stream bed. (Another fork in the path, a bit further on, also leads to the stream bed: in spring, if the stream is too full of water, keep to this upper path.) By either route, you will come to the HELLENISTIC BRIDGE shown overleaf (❼; **1h**), one of the highlights of this walk and an ideal spot for a shady rest — and another lovely setting for a picnic.

Just beyond the chapel on the east side of the bridge, take the right-hand, uphill fork, until you emerge on an old, pleasantly overgrown track. *(Unless it's blocked off, you could take another lovely diversion here, by turning left and following the track to where the valley opens out, and then returning to this point; see the map and allow 1h30min return — 3.4km, with a descent of 50m/165ft, followed by an ascent of 100m/325ft.)* The main walk turns *right* here, back towards the ridge of Archaia Eleftherna. You pass through a wire gate almost immediately, then join another track — the one you left earlier. Two sharp bends later you're back at the point where you took the path to the bridge.

Retrace your steps to the STEPPED PATH (❻) mentioned earlier (now on your left) and take it. After a minute the path turns right up some crude steps. It winds up the hillside, alternating between crude steps and flatter ground (from where you have good views over the valley). After about ten steep steps look for a red waymark on your left as the path flattens out. Turn sharp right at a large olive tree (also with a red waymark), ignoring the faint track going left uphill. Soon this flatter path begins to rise and become stepped.

When the path splits at some rustic wooden railings, take the uphill path to the left. (The downhill path to the right leads back to the NECROPOLIS.) From here it's just five minutes to the top (ignore a faint track heading right, downhill).

At the top you reach a small plateau (**1h30min**). The path keeps

Eleftherna's Byzantine tower

Hellenistic bridge

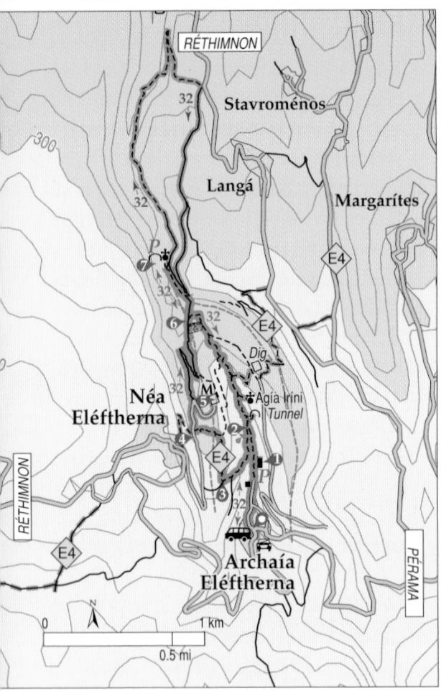

to the western edge of the ridge, but archaeological buffs may wish to explore the fenced acropolis excavation site ahead. To explore the ancient site, continue on the path following the western edge of the ridge. In four minutes take a small path climbing sharp left through a makeshift wire gate. There is a small ARCHAEOLOGICAL DIG on this plateau. Four minutes later, another sharp left turn leads to the next plateau, in the centre of which is the barrel-vaulted (roofless) church of **Agia Irini**. Returning to the main path, a couple of minutes further on you come to the last of the little surprises: another path climbs a bank on the left up to another plateau (only about 30m/yds wide). Cross to the far (eastern) side of it, to where you will find a path leading down to a 'ledge'. A few paces further on you will come to the entrance of an ANCIENT TUNNEL cut out of the rock. (A torch would come in handy here.) The entrance looks quite small, but the tunnel is surprisingly large once you are inside it. It was apparently used in ancient times to carry water from the cisterns to the dwellings on the eastern slope of the ridge.

But the main walk continues on the path for another 10 minutes or so, until regaining the CISTERNS at ❷. From here retrace your steps up the cobbled path, past the BYZANTINE TOWER (❶) and back to **Archaia Eleftherna** (**○**; **1h45min**).

BUS TIMETABLES

Bus times are *not* written in stone; seasonal changes are made in mid-May and mid-September. The timetables below represent the basic *summer* service ***in force pre-pandemic; buses are less frequent at present, but we hope they will return to these levels***. Extra buses run during the tourist season (May-Oct) for popular routes; buses are likely to be less frequent in spring and autumn. Check **www.e-ktel.com/en**, but it's wise to collect an up-to-date timetable from the bus station. Enquire about early-morning buses in particular if you think there is one (ie, if we have stated that there is one) because there's a chance they'll think you wouldn't dream of getting up at the crack of dawn when you're on holiday! Note, too, that there are other buses running from the resorts: ask for local timetables when you arrive. **Express buses** are unlikely to stop at intermediate destinations. See Index to locate quickly the timetable number for each destination; see pages 8-9 for bus stations.

BUSES FROM HANIA

1 Hania-Rethimnon; daily; journey 1h (continues to Iraklion; see Timetable 2 below)

Departures from Hania: 05.30, 06.30, 07.30, 08.30, 09.30, 10.30, 11.30, 12.00 (via the old road), 12.30, 13.30, 14.30, 15.30, 16.30, 17.30, 18.30, 19.30, 20.30. *Express: 08.45, 09.15, 11.15*

Departures from Rethimnon: 07.00, 07.30 (via the old road), 09.00, 10.00, 11.00, 12.00, 13.00, 14.00, 15.00, 16.00, 17.00, 18.00, 19.00, 20.00, 21.00, 22.00. *Express: 12.45, 13.45, 15.45*

2 Hania-Iraklion (via Rethimnon); daily; journey 2h

Departures from Hania: as Timetable 1 above

Departures from Iraklion: 05.30, 06.30, 07.30, 08.30, 09.30, 10.30, 11.30, 12.00 (via the old road), 12.30, 13.30, 14.30, 15.30, 16.30, 17.30, 18.30, 19.30, 20.30. *Express: 11.15, 12,15, 14.15*

3 Hania-Omalos; daily; journey about 45min

Departures from Hania: 06.15, 07.45, 08.45

Departures from Omalos: 07.30, 09.00, 13.30, 19.30

4 Hania-Hora Sfakion; daily; journey about 1h40min

Departures from Hania: 06.45, 08.15, 08.30, 11.00, 14.00, 16.00

Departures from Hora Sfakion: 07.00, 11.00, 13.30, 18.300

5 Hania-Paleohora; daily; journey 2h

Departures from Hania: 05.15, 08.45, 10.45, 12.45, 16.00, 20.00

Departures from Paleohora: 07.15, 12.00, 15.30, 18.15, 22.00

6 Hania-Sougia; daily; journey 1h45min

Departures from Hania: 05.00, 07.30 (Sundays only), 08.45, 13.45, 16.00

Departures from Sougia: 07.00 (Sundays only), 12.30, 18.30

7 Hania-Kolimbari; daily; journey 40min

Departures from Hania: 06.30, 07.15, 07.30, 08.00, 08.30, 09.00, 09.30, 10.00, 11.00, 11.30, 12.00, 12.30, 13.00, 13.15, 13.30, 14.00, 14.30, 15.00, 15.30, 16.30, 17.30, 18.00, 18.30, 19.30, 20.30, 21.00, 21.30, 22.00, 22.30, 23.00

Departures from Kolimbari: 05.15, 06.15, 07.15, 07.30, 08.00, 08.30, 09.00, 09.30, 10.00, 10.25, 11.10, 11.00, 11.30, 12.00, 12.30, 13.00, 13.30, 14.00, 14.10, 14.30, 15.00, 15.30, 16.00, 16.10, 17.10, 18.40, 18.50, 19.30, 20.30, 21.15, 21.40, 22.05

8 Hania-Kastelli-Kissamos; daily; journey 1h25min

Departures from Hania: 06.30, 07.15 (not Sat, Sun), 07.30 (only Sat, Sun), 08.30, 10.00, 11.00, 12.00, 13.00, 13.30 (only Sat, Sun), 14.30, 15.30, 16.30 (not Sat, Sun), 17.30, 18.30, 19.30, 20.30

Departures from Kastelli-Kissamos: 06.00, 07.00, 07.30 (not Sat, Sun), 08.00, 08.30, 09.30, 10.30, 11.30, 12.30, 14.00, 15.30, 16.30, 17.30, 18.30, 19.15

9 Hania–Kato Stalos–Agia Marina–Platanias–Maleme; daily

Departures from Hania: 06.30, 07.15, 08.00, 08.45 and every 15min until 11.00; 11.00 and every 30min until 23.00

Departures from Maleme Beach Hotel: 06.30, 07.15, 07.35, 07.55, 08.20, 08.45, 09.00 and every 15min until 11.15; 11.30 and every 30min until 22.00

10 Hania–Elafonisi (and Moni Chrisoskalitisas); daily; journey 1h15min

Departures from Hania: 09.00; *Departures from Elafonisi:* 16.00

BUSES FROM RETHIMNON

11 Rethimnon–Plakias; daily; journey 40min

Departures from Rethimnon: 05.30 (Mon-Fri *only*), 09.00, 11.00, 14.30, 18.00

Departures from Plakias: 07.00 (Mon-Fri *only*), 10.00, 12.00, 15.15, 19.00

12 Rethimnon–Hania; daily; journey 1h

Departures from Rethimnon; Departures from Hania: See Timetable 1

13 Rethimnon–Iraklion; daily; journey 1h30min

Departures from Rethimnon: 06.30, 07.30 (via the old road), 07.45, 08.30, 08.45, 09.15, 09.45, 10.15, 10.45, 11.15, 11.45, 12.15, 12.45, 13.15, 13.45, 14.00, 14.15, 14.45, 15.15, 15.45, 16.15, 16.45, 17.15, 17.45, 18.15, 18.45, 19.45, 20.45, 21.45. ***Express:* *09.45, 10.15, 12.15***

Departures from Iraklion: See Timetable 2

14 Rethimnon–Preveli; daily; journey 40min

Departures from Rethimnon: 09.00, 11.00, 14.30

Departures from Preveli: 11.30, 14.30, 18.30

15 Rethimnon–Asomatos–Plakias; daily; journey 40min

Departures from Rethimnon: 06.15 (not Sat, Sun), 10.00, 14.15, 16.30

Departures from Plakias: 07.00, 09.00 (only Sat, Sun), 11.45, 15.00, 18.00

16 Rethimnon–Hora Sfakion; daily; journey 1h30min

Departures from Rethimnon: 08.00, 14.15 (not Sat, Sun)

Departures from Hora Sfakion: 11.00 (not Sat, Sun), 17.30, 19.00

17 Rethimnon–Omalos; daily; journey 2h30min

Departures from Rethimnon: 06.15, 07.00

Departures from Omalos: via Hania; see Timetable 3 above

18 Rethimnon–Eleftherna; daily; journey 1h

Departures from Rethimnon: 06.15, 10.30, 12.45

Departures from Eleftherna: 07.00, 11.05, 16.00

19 Rethimnon–Timbaki–Mires (for Kamares); Mon-Fri; journey 1h30min-2h

Departure from Rethimnon: 07.00; *Departure from Kamares:* 13.50

20 Rethimnon–Mixorouma–Spili–Agia Galini; daily; journey 1h30

Departure from Rethimnon: 07.00, 10.30, 14.15

Departure from Mixorouma: 10.00, 12.30, 14.30, 16.30 (Mon-Fri), 09.00, 12.30, 16.30 (Sat/Sun); ***recheck departure times from Mixorouma in advance!***

BUSES FROM KASTELLI-KISSAMOS (see also Timetable 8 above)

21 Kastelli–Hania–Omalos; daily; journey 3h

Departures from Kastelli-Kissamos: 05.00, 06.00, 07.00, 14.00

Departures from Omalos: via Hania; see Timetable 3 above

22 Kastelli–Hania–Hora Sfakion; daily; journey 3h45min

Departures from Kastelli-Kissamos: via Hania; see Timetables 4 and 8

Departures from Hora Sfakion: 17.30

Index

Geographical names comprise the only entries in this Index. For other entries, see Contents, page 3. A page number in *italic type* indicates a map reference; a page number in **bold type** indicates a photograph. Both of these may be in addition to a text reference on the same page. Bus timetables are on pages 133-134.